gate to life

gate to life

You Choose the Life that You Shall Experience

Latresa Rice

220 Publishing

Chicago, Illinois
220 Publishing
(A Division of 220 Communications)

Published by 220 Publishing
(A Division of 220 Communications)
PO Box 8186
Chicago, IL 60680-8186
www.220communications.com
www.twitter.com/220publishing

Graphic design and inside layout by Julie M. Holloway
www.jmhcre8ive.com

Any people depicted in stock imagery provided by Thinkstock are models, and such images are being used for illustrative purposes only. Certain stock imagery © Thinkstock.

Because of the dynamic nature of the Internet, any web addresses or links contained in this book may have changed since publication and may no longer be valid. The views expressed in this work are solely those of the author and do not necessarily reflect the views of the publisher, and the publisher hereby disclaims any responsibility for them. All events and situations are accurate according to the author's knowledge.

CONTENTS

FOREWORD

Around the Christmas holiday 2013, I had the pleasure of meeting a wonderful young lady as a result of learning more of the process of publishing my own autobiography, "Starting from Scratch". Latresa was very knowledgeable, articulate, and full of positive energy. I would have never known, had she not shared, that she was the survivor of what are really near insurmountable circumstances. She was orphaned as a young girl at the age of seven as a result of losing her mother to AIDS. A couple of years later, she experienced traumatic abuse in her life.

Feeling unprotected and needing to survive, she quickly learned that she could show no weakness and took matters into her own hands to survive in a neighborhood plagued with drug dealers and gangs. In the city of Detroit, where approximately fifty percent live below the poverty line and less than half of students graduate with a high school diploma, Latresa learned to cope by keeping a scowl on her face while keeping people at a distance. No child should have to deal with these circumstances, so it is understandable that she would be filled with anger, fear, sadness, and an overall feeling that the world was against her.

It would have been an easy excuse for anyone to become an adverse statistic, but not Latresa. She realized that she could exercise her ability to choose another path. She worked hard in high school to get excellent grades, sold personalized poems to teachers to pay senior dues, and worked at a fast-food restaurant to pay for her prom dress. When she learned she would have no funding for college, she utilized success principles by seeking out the best strategies from counselors to receive scholarships which she earned to attend the University of Michigan. Afterwards, she also earned her Master's Degree, and became an ordained minister.

Many give up on at-risk youth like Latresa, and the few of those that make it out of these circumstances turn their back on these youth. I'm impressed that Latresa dedicated her life and has allowed God to use her story to reach back and inspire the most vulnerable of our society, the children experiencing similar issues. She understands that these youth are not throwaways, but are dealing with masked pain. Their negative behaviors are a cry for help for the hurt they feel on the inside, but have not learned positive methods to cope.

I am also greatly concerned with the plight of these economically disadvantaged youth as well. I was one myself growing-up in the projects of the south-Side of Ypsilanti, but by the grace of God have been fortunate to start several businesses, one employing over 3,000 employees and managing over 1 Billion dollars in client funds. While both Latresa and I come from impoverished backgrounds, the very essence and moral fabric, pride for oneself and community has been greatly diminished from when I was raised. This needs to change.

Some similarities are that we both value hard work, learned the value of entrepreneurship by necessity at an early age, believe in Gods power to change lives, and both took the Dale Carnegie Course to better ourselves.

It is my hope that economically disadvantaged youth are able to experience the success principles we learned in this course to continuously grow and develop ourselves. Also, they would greatly benefit from learning how to choose the "Gate to Life" which Latresa demonstrates in this book so that they can live the life they choose to experience.

Limits the Sky,

John W. Barfield,

Chairman Emeritus of Bartech Group

INTRODUCTION

As I stood on the playground, holding my baseball bat and eagerly awaiting my turn to hit the baseball, I turned to look at the pitcher as he prepared to send the ball in my direction. Suddenly, one of my second grade classmates, Erica, tapped me on the shoulder and said "Nisha is about to fight your sister!"

Instantly, I dropped the bat and followed her to the location where my sister was standing, actively engaged in an argument with Nisha.

Nisha was a dark-skinned girl who appeared to be at least 5'6" tall in the second grade. Before receiving this "breaking news" report from Erica, I hadn't had a problem with Nisha. However, today things had changed.

As the adrenaline pumped through my veins, I pushed through the crowd of gawking students, in order to defend my sister. While my sister, Korena, was still using every curse word imaginable to tell Nisha how she truly felt about her, I pushed her out of the way. Then, I jumped as high as I could and began to hit Nisha with my left and right fists. I continued to thrash her until the principal grabbed us both.

Sitting in the main office, fuming over what just took place, I threatened Nisha by saying, "If I get in trouble, you will get another beating."

Afterwards, Principal Thomas called us into her office to discuss the events surrounding the fight. As required by the school, she called both of our parents to inform them that we had been suspended for fighting.

My grandmother, Grandma Kali, received the call and promptly arranged for my great aunt to pick me up from school. Her name was Aunt Catherine. When she arrived, the first thing she said was, "Did you beat her up?" I replied, "Yes." "Then it's ok," my Aunt Catherine said. "You had to do what you had to do. You don't let nobody beat up your sister. You always take care of your family."

Later on that day, Grandma Kali arrived home. I already knew that I was about to get a whipping, but I didn't expect what happened next. Before the whipping, she asked, "Why were you fighting in school today?" Knowing that my response would have no effect on her decision to physically discipline me, I responded by rolling my eyes and spinning my head in a 360 degree motion as if it were a disc on an old record player.

Finally, I verbally responded to the question by saying, "Because the girl tried to fight my sister." After I said that, Grandma Kali said her famous words to me: "Don't be stupid all your life! At some point get a clue."

Needless to say, I was pissed! I thought she was calling me stupid so I said to her, "Grandma, you just called me stupid!" She said, "Don't put words in my mouth. I said, 'Don't be stupid all of your life.' What you did today was really stupid. Now you are suspended and your sister is still able to go to school. You need to think sometimes! But I'm going to help you think by giving you something to think about. Each time you do something stupid like this, you will get a whipping." Immediately, she whipped me with her belt. The more she whipped me, the angrier I became. After the whipping, I had to sit in my room for 10-15 minutes. Once the time was over, I was able to go outside to play. Instead of playing, I walked the neighborhood to calm down. Typically people in the neighborhood would be laughing, and I would assume that they were laughing at me. Because I thought they must have been laughing at me, I would walk towards them and prepare to "defend myself" by fighting. Every time I was caught fighting, Grandma Kali would say, "Don't be stupid all your life! At some point, get a clue."

This cycle continued until 10th grade. However, it wasn't until I became an adult that I finally realized what my grandmother's statement truly meant.

This book depicts my life as a young child through young adulthood, revealing the various barriers that I faced, and how I overcame them to accomplish my dreams.

Life presents us with many different gates. It's up to us to use our keys to open the gate that leads to the life we desire. In order to do this, we must think about all the possible consequences of our actions before we act. For every action, there is a reaction; however, we can choose the type of reactions that we desire to experience. With God, all things are possible. If we ask Holy Spirit to empower and direct us, we can make the right choices. You choose the life that you shall experience!

CHAPTER 1

MASKED PAIN: FROM ELEMENTARY TO MIDDLE

Elementary Experiences

Dunt! Dunt! Dunt! Dunt! Dunt! Dunt! Was the loud annoying sound that I heard each morning at 6:00 am. We had recently moved into Grandma Kali's house following my mother's death and I was still not used to the sound of this alarm clock.

Each time it rang in this manner, I promptly responded to the annoyance by taking the palm of my hand and pounding on the snooze button until the sound ceased. Lying in silence, I thought to myself, "Ah, peace and quiet. Finally, I can get at least 10 minutes of sleep." I was wrong.

Within two minutes of hearing the alarm, Grandma Kali's ritual of yelling to me from the living room to my upstairs bedroom began. "Tresa! Get Up! It's time for school. I know you heard that alarm clock!" A minute later "Get up and get ready for school!" was repeated.

Grandma Kali is the name of my maternal grandmother. She is an African-American woman approximately 5'3" tall and thin in stature. She weighs approximately 110 pounds. To appease her, I'd lift my head above my pillow, yell "OK!" then lay back down to get a few more minutes of rest.

As I rested in bed with my eyes closed, the piercing sound of the alarm clock would go off again. By this time I was enraged and I would take the alarm clock, press the snooze button, and launch it onto the floor. BANG! Immediately following this banging sound, Grandma Kali would say "Girl, what the hell are you doing?" My response would be "Nothing grandma. I'm up." Grandma Kali went on, "then what the hell was that noise? I know it better not have been that alarm clock!" To refrain from lying, I'd keep silent, praying that she would not ask me again about the alarm clock.

After rising from bed, I had 30 minutes to bathe, get dressed, groom myself, eat breakfast, and then walk to school. Breakfast was typically the one item on my agenda that consistently got overlooked.

School Bully: I guess he didn't know me

Whether I ate breakfast or not, it was imperative that my brother, sister and I arrived on time at our new school, so we dashed out the door and walked to school.

As we walked to school, I couldn't help but think about my deceased mother that I missed so much. I thought to myself, "If God hadn't taken my mommy from me; I wouldn't have to even go to this school."

These thoughts subsided as we arrived at Nancy Lane Elementary School. There was a huge gravel playground located to the right, and a small grass playground located to the left.

I walked my sister and brother to the entrance next to the gravel playground, and then went to the entrance next to the grassy playground.

While in my 1st hour classroom, I discovered that students in kindergarten through second grade played on the playground with grass, and the students from third through fifth grade played on the gravel playground during recess.

I would think to myself, "I really don't want to go outside and be with these kids." As I transitioned from my 1st and 2nd hour classes, I knew that my recess time was approaching, which was right after math class.

Sitting quietly in my second grade math classroom, I thought to myself, "I don't want to go to this school. I miss my mom! Mom, why did you leave me here?" My thoughts were disturbed by the routine task of taking attendance.

"Latresa Rice," Ms. Handscreator said as she took attendance. I immediately replied, "Here!" Ms. Handscreator was my math teacher. She was a Caucasian American woman, approximately 5'11" tall with long blonde hair. Ms. Handscreator loved her students. Every day she would allow us to have the opportunity to earn a star.

In order to earn a star, you had to complete all of your class work, turn your homework in on time, or exhibit good behavior. At the end of the week, we could redeem our stars for prizes like candy, stickers, pencils, erasers etc.

As the new kid, I got accustomed to the glares and stares of the other students in the class. Ms. Handscreator would tell me how smart I was, but that she would love to see me participate more in class.

When we heard the sound of the recess bell, she would say to us, "Ok everyone, it's time for recess. Put away your things, clean up your area, push your chairs in, and then line up by the door."

The students in my class were so excited that they completed the required tasks within a matter of seconds, and then stood in line at the door.

Meanwhile, I was still sitting in my chair. One student in my class said, "Come on, it's time to go." I rolled my eyes at her and continued to take my time. If looks could kill, she would have died like a rat dies when poison is released into its blood stream. Ms. Handscreator did not notice my attitudinal response to the student. Instead, she continued to give orders to the class by saying, "All of you can start walking towards the playground." As the students obeyed the instructions, she walked over towards my desk and asked me a question.

"Latresa, is everything ok? Why is it taking you so long to get your things together so that you can go outside?" she asked.

"I don't want to go outside. I don't like any of the people here and I don't have any friends," I responded.

"You're still new at school, sweetie. You have to get to know people first before you say that you don't like them. You never know, you may like them later. Go outside and have some fun," said Ms. Handscreator. Immediately, I got up from my seat, packed up my things, pushed my chair in, exited the classroom, and walked to the playground.

The Playground Experience

While standing on the play ground, I saw kids swinging on the swings, climbing on the monkey bars, sliding down the slides, running, and enjoying themselves. Other children played games such as "Ring around the Roses," "Slide" and many more. You could hear the sound of laughter, as the kids engaged in their various interactive activities. I did not participate. Instead, I sat on the steps by the entrance to the building waiting for the teacher, principal, or any other administrator to call for us to come back into the building and go to class.

Sitting on the steps looking at the ground, I was shocked when a male student by the name of Edwin approached me. Edwin was a heavyset, dark-skinned kid who was known for having a bad attitude and bullying his fellow students in the second grade.

"Hey girl, give me your lunch money," he demanded. "No, it's mine. I suggest you get out my face!" I retorted. He laughed and reached for my backpack so that he could take my lunch money.

Subsequently, I was presented with two gates to choose from, with regards to how I could respond to this situation. Only one gate leads to a prosperous life. Some of the potential consequences related to each gate are listed below. Please review the descriptions of the gates and determine which gate you believe would lead to a life of prosperity. Are there any additional potential consequences related to each gate? Which gate do you believe I chose?

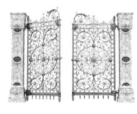 **Gate #1: Tell someone**

By informing the higher authorities, I could avoid unnecessary trouble such as suspension from school, getting a whipping when I get home, being placed on punishment etc.

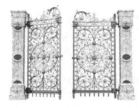 **Gate #2: Handle it my way . . . Fight**

By fighting, I would satisfy my fleshly desire to get revenge immediately, prove a point to others who may be thinking about harming me, etc.

Do you believe that you guessed the right gate that I chose? As you turn to the next page, my choice will be revealed. I chose . . .

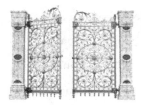 **Gate #2: Handle it my way . . . Fight**

In response, I bit into his wrist as if it were the last piece of chicken left during a famine. In order to ensure that no one could easily get his wrist away from me, I locked my teeth into it. He screamed! The louder he screamed, the deeper I sank my teeth into his wrist.

Within a matter of minutes, students and teachers surrounded us. The Assistant Principal grabbed me and attempted to pull me off of him. The harder she pulled me, the harder I bit him. Once she stopped pulling on me, I released his wrist from my deadly grip.

Afterwards, she marched us to the principal's office. Edwin was still crying about his wrist. I was so mad! In an attempt to calm down, I blew air in and out of my nostrils, as if I were a bull preparing to charge at an unsuspecting victim.

This breathing exercise helped me calm down enough to be able to avoid harming Edwin again, sit next to him, and wait to be called into the principal's office.

As I sat there waiting, I reflected on what I had recently heard another student say about Principal Thomas, when I was walking through the hall on my way to the main office. "Ms. Thomas is so mean that she beats kids with an electric paddle."

Suddenly my thoughts were interrupted as Principal Thomas approached us. She was a tall, thin, dark-skinned woman with a short trimmed afro hairstyle. "Follow me," she said. I remembered the electric paddle, and thought to myself, "I'm going to rip her face off if she tries to hit me with that."

Once we entered into Principal Thomas's office, she asked Edwin to explain what happened. Immediately he said that I bit him and would not let him go. He failed to inform her of the fact that he was trying to take my money.

After he finished explaining his position, she turned to me and asked me what happened.
I told her what happened in detail. However, regardless of the details, she did not seem amused or pleased with what had taken place on the playground.

Ms. Thomas took out her paddle. Much to my surprise, it was not an electric paddle. The paddle had a silver wire attached to the end of it which gave it the appearance of being an electric paddle.

She said that we were going to be suspended, and that she should beat us with the paddle. After hearing this remark, I said, "If you hit me with that paddle, I'm going to beat you up." "What did you just say little girl?" asked Ms. Thomas. "You not hitting me with that! If you do, I'm gone beat you up!" I replied. Ms. Thomas seemed shocked. So much so that she sent Edwin to class and then told me that she was calling my grandmother.

Instantly, I knew that I was in trouble again, yet I still murmured the word "so" under my breath.

Contacting Grandma:

Not Good

"So" was a comment that, if heard out of the mouth of a child, enraged most people in authority. Grandma Kali is one of those people.

With eyes as brown as a chocolate truffle, and hands as firm as a cast iron skillet, Grandma Kali is a force with insurmountable power. She could either cause you to be extremely glad, or extremely mad, by her responses to things that you did.

This was an extremely mad occasion. Although I knew nothing good could come out of the phone call home, I was too upset to even make an attempt to be respectful to Principal Thomas. As I sat in my seat staring at Ms. Thomas, all I could think of was what I was about to experience when I arrived home.

"I hope I get a whipping because afterwards I can go outside and play with my friends," I thought to myself. Then my thoughts were interrupted by Principal Thomas' voice as she said, "Here Ms. Rice, your grandmother would like to talk to you." Those words terrified me.

Holding back tears in order to still appear to be tough, I reached for the telephone receiver and in a soft tone I said hello.

"Girl, what the hell is wrong with you?" Grandma Kali demanded. "Nothing," I said in a sassy manner, full of attitude.

"Then why the hell are you up at that school actin a fool!" said Grandma Kali.

"He tried to steal my money!" I shouted, and Grandma Kali replied, "How many times have I told you that you need to tell somebody? You don't just do what you want to do. If I have to take off work and come up to that school because you actin a fool, I'm going to take you to the front of your class, beat your behind then make you apologize to everyone for interrupting their learning time. Do you hear me?" she asked. Although I hesitated to respond, my response was "yes".

"Now give the phone back to the principal," Grandma Kali said. Although I was pissed off, I sat back in my chair and thought to myself, "I can't believe he got me in trouble. I should kick his butt again since I'm already in trouble. Oooo, nobody bet not say nothin to me!"

Finally, I looked at Principal Thomas as she continued to converse with my grandmother. She said that I will be suspended from school for three days, and I needed someone to come pick me up from school. My grandmother told her that my great Aunt Catherine would come pick me up from school. Afterwards, the two of them ended the telephone conversation. I remained in the office until my Aunt Catherine arrived.

ARRIVAL HOME: NO CHANGE IN BEHAVIOR

If anyone could be a twin of Grandma Kali, it would be my great Aunt Catherine. Aunt Catherine was one of Grandma Kali's sisters. She was known as the "cool, laid back auntie."

Aunt Catherine was the mother of two children: Johan and Tony. Johan was 17 years younger than Tony. She was known to sell and use drugs. However, she had such a wonderful personality. Children could crack jokes and just have a blast with Aunt Catherine. Today was not any different.

Upon arriving to the school, Aunt Catherine entered the main office and signed for me to be released into her care. We exited the school and walked five blocks to get home. Because this was my first offense, I wasn't sure what to expect from Aunt Catherine. While we were walking home, she asked me, "What happened?" I was still upset, so I responded in the following manner with an elevated tone of voice, "This dumb boy tried to take my money, so I bit him!" "Ok, so why are you yelling? He did something to you and you beat him up right?"

I was shocked to hear those words come out of her mouth. I was expecting a good old fashion brow-beating, tongue-lashing. Instead I received what appeared to be approval of my conduct at school. I replied, "Yes".

"Well that's good, Aunt Catherine said. "You don't let nobody hurt you or your family. Do you hear me?" she asked. "Yes," I replied.

Unfortunately, I took the phrase "don't let nobody" literally; thus, whenever anyone hurt me emotionally or physically, or any member of my family, I was fighting.

My decision to fight in response to the offense was not dependent upon whether the offender was a relative or a stranger. It didn't matter. I meditated on what Aunt Catherine had told me.

However, approximately four hours later I heard the following sound: SLAM! This was the sound of the front door. My sister, brother, and cousins had arrived home. They ran upstairs to the bedroom where we all typically gathered. This time I was occupying that room and did not want any company. "Did you get suspended?" Korena asked.

"What does it look like?" I shouted.

"You ain't got to get no attitude. I was just asking yo dumb butt a question!"

"Don't say nothing else to me!" I replied.

"I can say what I want to say. You don't tell me what to do. You ain't my momma!" Korena yelled at the top of her lungs.

My sister's response upset me. However, while in the midst of angry emotions; I found myself standing before two gates: each bearing their own set of consequences.

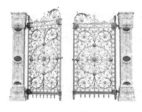

Gate # 1: Ignore her.

By ignoring her, I could avoid getting into any more trouble.

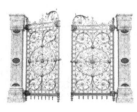

Gate # 2: React on the primitive thought that was running through my mind . . . Fight.

By fighting her, I risked being put on punishment, getting a whipping, harming her significantly, or possibly getting harmed.

Can you think of any other potential consequences from choosing either Gate #1 or Gate #2? Which gate do you believe I chose? Which gate would you choose? Why would you make that choice? Which gate is the best choice? As you turn to the next page, you will discover my selection.

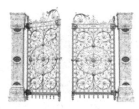 **Gate # 2: React on the primitive thought running through my mind . . . Fight.**

Immediately, I jumped off the bed and physically attacked Korena. She threw things at me, but she missed. Next I charged at her with the force of a mad horse.

Finally the fight was dismantled by Aunt Catherine, after she engaged in a marathon dash upstairs and entered our bedroom.

"Y'all need to cut that mess out! That's the only sister you got!" she stated. Korena looked at me and rolled her eyes as if she were rolling two basketballs around on the tips of her index fingers. With my lips pressed and sealed shut, I looked at Korena and returned her glaring stare and eye rolling technique. Our death lock stares were interrupted by the sound of Grandma Kali's voice yelling up the stairs, as she entered the house from work.

"TRESA! KORENA! COME HERE!!"
Grandma Kali commanded. "Ok!" We yelled in unison
as if we were a choir.

We ran down the stairs and entered the front
room. I thought to myself, "What now?" Then, my
thoughts were interrupted by Grandma Kali's statement.

"Aunt Catherine told me that y'all were fighting
before I got here. What the hell is wrong with y'all?"
Grandma Kali demanded.

"Nothing," I replied while Korena continued to
stand there looking like a little tea pot with steam rising
out of its spout.

"The next time you two fight each other, I'm
gone whip both of you. Do you hear me?"

"Yes," I replied while Korena just stood there
nodding her head. "And Tresa, the next time you show
yo butt up there at that school, I'm going to come up
there, take you in front of your class, whip your butt and
make you apologize for disturbing the other students
class time. Do you hear me?" she threatened. "Yes," I
replied.

After replying "yes," both Korena and I were allowed to go outside to play with the rest of my relatives and friends; but things got worse.

I couldn't seem to calm down, so I took a walk through the neighborhood. Huffing and puffing with my fist clinched tighter than the lid on a can of sweet peas, I stomped through the neighborhood. Sights of people laughing and having fun made me sick to my stomach. I thought to myself, "What's so funny?" I asked some strangers who were laughing this question: "What the hell are you laughing at?" They looked at me as if I were insane, or replied to the question in their own manner. If I didn't like their responses, I would walk over to that person and tell them that if they said it again, I would "blow their mouth out." Most people either ignored me or told me to get out of their face and walked away.

I continued my walk. After walking a block and a half, I finally calmed down enough to go back towards the house and enjoy playing with my friends.

CHAPTER 2

SUMMER TIME

Playing with my female friends involved going on "journeys," dancing in the driveway, racing up and down the block, climbing trees, making mud pies, and throwing water balloons. However, playing with my male friends involved more physical activities. It was not unusual for me to be found playing football, baseball, basketball, or wrestling with the boys in my neighborhood.

Since it was Friday and it was nice outside, my female friends and I went on a "journey". We defined a "journey" as an event in which three or more of the youth on our block got together and walked or rode our bikes all over the neighborhood, stopped at parks or visited a friend's house to play cards, and sports, such as basketball, football etc. Journeys were only taken during the summer months. In order to go on a "journey" we had to do the following:

1.   Tell someone. Although we didn't have to tell Grandma Kali exactly where we were going, we did have to tell her or someone residing within the home that we were going on a "journey".

2.   Get our bikes ready or prepare to walk. If we chose to ride bikes, we would all get our bikes and line them up at either Victoria's, Carissa's, or my house. If we chose to walk, we would make sure we packed enough water bottles for our journey. Approximately thirteen children would get together and travel throughout the neighborhood, visiting the liquor stores, the penny candy store, playgrounds, and schools within the area.

3.   Pack lunches for everyone traveling and bring an extra lunch for someone who we may run into along the way that might be hungry. To prepare for our journey, we planned ahead and made at least one extra sandwich per person. Therefore, if any of us were still hungry or if we met someone while at the playground who said that he / she was hungry, we could give them something to eat while we all ate our lunches.

4.   Bring additional items for outdoor activities. Sometimes we brought a basketball, football, water guns, baby dolls, trucks etc. on the journey, to ensure that we could do whatever we decided to do as a group.

After completing the necessary stages of preparation for our journey, we voyaged to Nancy Lane Elementary School. Knowing the importance of sticking together, we voted with regards to what side of the school we would play on: the majority vote won. Usually we chose to play on the side of the building where the swing set was located. We called this side of the building "the park".

Sounds of laughter and joyful screams filled the air as we played and enjoyed ourselves at "the park". We termed this side of the building "the park" because it was the side that had grass, monkey bars, swing sets, slides, and much more. Although there were actual parks within the area, we rarely went to those parks because drug dealers, alcoholics, and others were present at those parks and they made us feel uncomfortable.

As the sky changed colors, from a pastel blue to a grayish blue, we knew that the street lights would come on soon, so we traveled back to our various destinations.

After walking my friends to their homes, Korena, Daeon, April, Johan, Kathy and I arrived at

Grandma Kali's house. On the weekends, we were allowed to stay awake as long as we desired, but often each of us were so exhausted from our journey that we decided to go to sleep early.

Lying in my twin-sized bed in a room surrounded by blue walls, I folded my two pillows in half, pulled my blanket over my slim frame and drifted off to sleep.

Recurrent Nightmare

"You can't get me! You can't get me!" Timina, Nolan, Delane, Mia, other cousins and I all yelled, as a man with a blank face grabbed us one by one and threw us onto the bed.

Laughing hysterically, we faintly heard him tell us that he was tired, so he instructed everyone to leave the room and go downstairs. Like wild oxen, we stampeded out of the room, but I was caught in the grasp of the one who caused the stampede: the blank- faced man.

"Tresa, you can stay in here with me," declared the blank-faced man. Then he placed me onto the bed.

"Did you know that you are my favorite niece?" he asked.

"No," I replied.

"Well, you are and you are so beautiful. Your mother was just as beautiful as you are," declared the blank-faced man. I smiled. Then he asked me to come closer to him. As an obedient child, I honored his request.

After getting closer to the blank-faced man, I smelled a horrible stench protruding from his mouth and skin. It was as if someone took all the liquor and wine available in the country and poured it down his throat.

"Do you want to play another game?" he asked. With excitement I said, "Yes!"

He said "Let's play house. I'm the father and you're the mother. Now lie down." I complied. Immediately, the blank-faced man positioned himself on top of me. He kissed me on my neck. Then he put one of his hands on my butt and placed the other hand into my pants while I laid there trying not to throw up. I was so terrified that I couldn't yell. Then the blank-faced man looked into my eyes and jumped off of me as if he had seen a ghost.

Much to my surprise, it was only a nightmare. Immediately I sat in an upright position, shivering, dripping with sweat, and gripping my baby doll, as I thought about the events that occurred within the nightmare.

While awake, I soon noticed that all the lights were out. I was so afraid of the dark that I walked to the bathroom and turned on the lights. Afterwards, I went back to my bedroom and drifted to sleep again.

A Typical Summer Day

The next morning, I was awakened by Carissa, who stood by the edge of my bed and said, "Get up, sleepyhead!"

"What up doe? When you get here?" I asked, as I yawned and wiped the crust from the corners of my eyes.

"Don't worry bout dat, GET CHO BUTT UP AND GET DRESSED!" she said while looking at me and laughing.

"Aight den, dats what it be like, I'm getting up," I answered back.

Carissa was my best friend. She and I went everywhere together. We were what you call "Ride or Die" friends. That meant that if she needed anything, I'd do my best to get it for her and vice versa. Carissa was approximately two inches taller than I, dark-skinned, and thin. Over the years, Carissa and I noticed that we had many things in common.

For example, the same year that my mother died, Carissa's father died. We both experienced some sort of inappropriate touching at the hands of someone who was either in or close to our families. We were also known to have tempers.

On this particular day, we decided to go outside and go to Victoria's house. While at Victoria's house we played music, danced in the driveway, and made frequent trips to the penny candy store. Our activities outside Victoria's house were frequently interrupted by a rude remark or action committed by the grandchildren of Victoria's neighbors.

"Y'all need to shut up! With y'all ugly butts!" Monte yelled. Immediately, everyone engaged in a verbal battle with him. "I know he ain't talkin to me!" I stated. "Yeah, I'm talkin to you, you ugly girl!" "You Ugly!" I replied. "Yo momma ugly!" he retorted.

At that moment, I was presented with a choice.

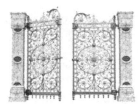 **Gate #1: Ignore him and continue to enjoy my time with my friends.**

By ignoring him, I would be able to retain control of the situation; thus, enjoy my time with my friends.

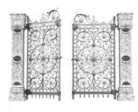 **Gate #2: Make an example out of him by thrashing him over and over again until he is bleeding profusely.**

By beating him up, I would be able to express my displeasure with regards to his rude remarks and ensure that he and others would remember how I felt about those remarks for years to come. In resorting to this action, I would run the risk of getting a whipping or being put on punishment.

Which gate do you believe I chose? Can you think of any other consequences related to choosing either of the two gates? Which gate would you choose and why?

What do you believe would happen to you as a result of choosing that gate? As you turn to the next page, you will discover which gate I chose to walk through.

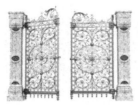 **Gate #2: Make an example out of him by thrashing him over and over again until he is bleeding profusely.**

By beating him up, I would be able to express my displeasure with regards to his rude remarks and ensure that he and others would remember how I felt about those remarks for years to come. In resorting to this action, I would run the risk of getting a whipping or being put on punishment.

Feeling as if steam was blowing out of the top of my head, I jumped off the porch and dashed towards Monte. Monte's two older brothers, Junior and Antonio, ran towards me and fought me for him. I equally dispersed an array of successful punches amongst the boys. Korena, Victoria, Carissa, and several other close friends and relatives stood to the side to watch the brawl. While I was fighting the two brothers, Monte went into the house and got his grandmother, Ms. Ruthy.

Standing about 5'5" tall, Ms. Ruthy looked like a skyscraper standing next to me. She was thin and several of her teeth were missing.

Ms. Ruthy and my grandmother were good friends. Every day they went to the Bingo hall together.

After being warned of the brawl that was taking place outside, Ms. Ruthy came storming out of the home towards me.

Instead of grabbing her two grandsons, she grabbed me. I was so enraged that I punched her in the mouth, as if I were a professional boxer, and continued to batter her two grandchildren. Eventually, she was able to get her two grandchildren into the house and I went home.

While sitting in my bedroom attempting to calm down, I heard a knock at the door.

"Who is it?" Grandma Kali asked.

"Ruthy!" replied Ms. Ruthy.

Then Grandma Kali opened the front door and said, "Hey, how are you? Is everything ok?"

"No," replied Ms. Ruthy.

"Tresa was out here fighting my two grandsons. When I tried to break up the fight, she punched me in the face!"

As I actively "ear-hustled," I heard this conversation and thought to myself, "Nothing good can come out of this."

"Tresa!" Grandma Kali yelled.

"Yes!" I replied.

"Get down here!" shouted Grandma Kali.

With my heart racing, and the adrenaline in my body steadily flowing like a stream of water from a brook, I dashed out of my bedroom and ran down the stairs towards the living room.

"Tresa, why did you punch Ms. Ruthy in the face?" demanded Grandma Kali.

"Because her grandkids talked about my momma and were trying to beat me up," I explained.

"Instead of grabbing them, she tried to grab me," I went on.

"I thought she was trying to hold me and let her grandkids beat me up!"

"Don't be stupid all your life. That is real stupid! You know better than that. You don't put your hands on anyone, let alone on an adult. Apologize right now!" Grandma Kali demanded.

"No, it's her own fault that she got punched. She shouldn't have tried to put her hands on me!"

At that moment, Grandma Kali appeared to be as red as a cherry. Her eyes narrowed and the hairs on her skin appeared to be standing as soldiers ready for battle. She slapped me and said, "Girl, I said apologize. Do it now!"

Huffing and puffing, I answered with a loud "NO!!"

Fully aware of the consequences of this response, and because I was upset about being slapped, I decided to continue to speak my mind.

"I'm going to beat the mess out of them the next time I see them!" I yelled at the top of my lungs.

Grandma Kali stopped attempting to force me to apologize to Ms. Ruthy, turned towards her and said, "This child done lost her mind. I apologize for her actions. It won't happen again."

Ms. Ruthy said ok and departed from our home. Now Grandma Kali and I were left standing at the door. As she turned towards me she said, "Get out of my face! Go to your room and think about what you did! You not going back outside until I say so," she said angrily.

Envisioning her head underneath my foot, I stomped as I walked to my room.

"Stomp one more time here!" yelled Grandma Kali.

I waited until I got to my room, took the door knob out of the door, and stomped on the floor repeatedly as hard as I could.

Of course Grandma Kali was pissed. She stormed up the stairs and tried to get into the bedroom.

Realizing that she couldn't get in because I had taken the door knob out of the door, she banged on the door and said, "Open this door and you better open it now!" I refused to open the door.

Less than five minutes later, she had gotten a butter knife from downstairs and opened the door herself. Immediately she gave me a whipping and then went downstairs. I thought to myself, "Yes! A whipping, I will surely be able to go back outside now." After approximately ten minutes, Grandma Kali came up to talk to me.

"Tresa, you don't fight folks because they talk about you or your momma. People will talk about you all your life. Just ignore them. You gotta learn how to control your anger or you will end up dead or in jail."

Looking at her with tears in my eyes, I asked Grandma Kali, "What did my mommy die from?"

"Pneumonia," she replied.

Her response caused me to be upset all over again because I thought about the fact that my brother, sister and I were not allowed to go to my mother's funeral.

My silence was broken once Grandma Kali said, "You can go back outside, but I better not hear about you gettin into any more fights."

"OK," I replied, knowing full well that my agreement wasn't true.

Because I was dealing with rage, getting a whipping accelerated my anger. As I walked outside I thought to myself, "I'm going to take a walk because I am pissed. If anybody says something to me or about me it's on!"

Needless to say, I was fighting again. This pattern continued throughout the summer.

BACK TO SCHOOL

At last, summer was over and it was time to gain more knowledge. The thought of learning new things was invigorating for me. However, the fact that I would have to socialize with "the people" caused me to desire to stay home and lock myself in my bedroom with books written by Nancy Thomas readily at my disposal.

"The people" were those who ridiculed, mocked, teased, or behaved in a rude manner towards me or someone else in my presence.

"The people" were uncaring, inconsiderate, disrespectful, and ungrateful with regards to how they treated me or those I loved. "The people" were also known as "haters".

While returning to school, what I didn't want to experience happened. I had to deal with a member of "the people". This member was not a student. It was a teacher.

As I sat in the classroom pondering what I was going to say when called upon to present "My desired position" assignment, I decided that I would tell everyone that I desired to become the first African-American president of the United States of America.

I watched as many other students said that they wanted to become doctors, lawyers, football players, basketball players and teachers. Suddenly, my name was called.

"Latresa Rice," said Ms. Cannerage. With a notebook in my hand, I sashayed to the front of the room and proclaimed to the class what I wanted to become when I grew up and my plan to make my dream a reality.

As I stood up straight, I held my head up high and said, "When I grow up, I'm going to be the president of the United States of America."

Before I could finish my presentation, Ms. Cannerage interrupted me.

"Ok that's nice, but I need you to think of a more realistic career. You will never be the president of the United States of America because first of all, you are black. Second of all, you are a female," she said.

"Is there anything else that you would like to be when you grow up?" she blurted.

As those words slid out of her mouth, I felt as if my dream was being annihilated by some lunatic with a semi-automatic rifle. Immediately, I retaliated. "Watch Me!" I said in the most sassy, attitudinal tone I could muster.

"Excuse me Ms. Rice, What did you say?" Ms. Cannerage responded.

Rolling my eyes like two marbles being twirled on a table top, I replied "You heard me, I said, Watch me!"

Ms. Cannerage arose from her seat, rushed towards me and grabbed my arm.

"GET YOUR HANDS OFF OF ME!" I yelled. Yelling at her did not work as a method to get her to release me.

Instead, Ms. Cannerage placed another one of the students in charge of the class and promptly marched me down to the principal's office.

"What's wrong now?" Principal Thomas asked.

"Ms. Rice was being disrespectful and insubordinate in my class this morning," stated Ms. Cannerage.

Principal Thomas shook her head and said, "I'll take care of this Ms. Cannerage. Go ahead and go back to your class."

Desiring to blow both Principal Thomas and Ms. Cannerage down like the wolf in the story titled "The Three Little Pigs" blew down each of the houses of the pigs; I sat on the bench with my fist balled up and blew air out of my nostrils like an enraged bull.

"So Ms. Rice, you are back in my office again?" the principal asked.

"Yes I am," I said.

"What happened this time?"

"I was talking about what I wanted to be when I grew up and the teacher was rude to me, so then I was rude to her."

"Tell me, how she was rude to you. Tell me the whole story," inquired Principal Thomas.

"I said that I wanted to be the president of the United States of America when I grow up, and she said that I needed to be more realistic because it would never happen since I'm black and I'm a female. After she said that, then I told her to WATCH ME!"

"I'll talk to Ms. Cannerage about that, but you have to learn how to control your anger. Just because someone is rude to you doesn't mean that you have to be rude to them. She is an adult," Principal Thomas stated.

"Whatever!" I yelled as I sat back on the bench.

"You will be getting a letter sent home to your grandma and I will be calling her."

"So," I mumbled under my breath.

"Because it is almost time for you to go to your next class, you can stay here until the bell rings, then take all of your things and go to class."

I did not respond. I was so upset that I sat there cracking my knuckles and waiting for the sound of the bell. After 15 minutes, the bell sounded. I dashed out of the office and went to class.

Although I didn't get into any more trouble in school that day, I knew that responding to the principal in that manner was not a good idea. I thought to myself, "Maybe I should take my time going back home. After all, there is no need for me to rush home."

In fact, it would be best for me to take my time traveling home, since that would probably be the most enjoyment I would get today.

At that moment, I made the decision to take my brother and sister on the long route home, as opposed to taking the shortest route to our house. After all, this was the last day of the school year, and it was best that I at least enjoyed this momentary excitement before getting home.

As we walked home, I thought to myself, "I am in trouble, but I am so glad that it's summer time again!"

Home Sweet Home

I walked with my brother, sister, and cousins in a zigzag pattern towards the house, passing through the neighborhood rather than walking straight down James Street and making a left on Country Lane Rd. This journey home took us approximately 30 minutes instead of our usual 15 minutes.

Much to my surprise, no one was at the house when we arrived. However, we always knew that there was someone who would be held accountable for any of our inappropriate behavior exhibited. In fact, Grandma Kali always designated someone to be in charge, if an adult was not present.

In order to be in charge, you had to be the oldest child. Grandma Kali ran her household in a military fashion. In fact, there was always a chain of command in place if she was not at the house.

First in command was Aunt Leah. Aunt Leah was approximately 5' 6" tall with short black hair. She had one daughter named April. I was second in command.

Because Aunt Leah was not home, I was in charge. Recognizing my responsibility and knowing that we were told to have the house clean by the time Grandma Kali arrived home, I took on the role of "general" and gave commands to all the "privates" residing in the home.

"Daeon, clean the kitchen. Korena clean the bathroom. April help Korena clean the bathroom and I will clean the front room," I commanded.

"You not my momma! You don't tell me what to do!" yelled Korena.

"Grandma Kali told me that the only thing that I have to do is take out the trash," stated Daeon.

"I don't want to clean up the bathroom," stated April.

I thought about all of their remarks then retorted, "Grandma Kali said that this house better be clean before she gets here today, and that I am in charge whenever there isn't an adult present. So, do what I said, or else."

"I ain't doing nothin and you can't make me!" yelled Korena.

"I'm telling Grandma!" yelled my brother Daeon, as he went into the kitchen to clean it.

"I'm telling my momma!" yelled my cousin April, as she went upstairs to clean the bathroom.

Both Daeon and April proceeded to follow my instructions; however, Korena was rebellious.

"Korena, go help April clean up the bathroom like I said!" I yelled.

"You don't tell me what to do. NO! I'm going outside!" yelled Korena as she walked towards the door.

Steaming mad, I rushed towards Korena, pushed her and said, "Do what I said to do!"

She was not pleased with my actions. Korena pushed me back. One thing led to another, and then we fought each other.

"I hate you!" yelled Korena, as she stormed up the stairs. "I hate you too!" I retorted.

Somehow, Grandma Kali found out about the fight. When she arrived home, she placed her purse on the couch.

"TRESA and KORENA!" she yelled. "Yes?" we answered from upstairs.

"Why were you two fighting?" "What is wrong with y'all?" asked Grandma Kali.

"I told her to help April clean the bathroom and she said NO," I replied.

With her arms folded and rolling her eyes, Korena replied, "So what, you not my momma."

Listening intently to the tone of her voice, I knew that we were in trouble. I walked down the stairs with caution.

"When I am not here and no one else is here, Tresa is in charge. Anyway, I told all of y'all that I wanted this house cleaned by the time I got home, so it doesn't matter who said to clean it, I expect it to be done. Do you hear me?"

"Yes," we each replied.

"Tresa, keep your hands to yourself. You don't put your hands on nobody. This is the only sister you have. The next time you put your hands on her, I am going to put my hands on you. That goes for the both of you. Do you hear me?"

"Yes."

"Now go outside and play. Soon summer will be over and you all will have to get ready for the new school year, so you need to avoid getting in trouble and just enjoy the summer," Grandma Kali stated.

"Ok," we replied.

"Can I go over Carissa's house?"

"Yes, make sure you are in front of this house by the time the street lights come on."

"Yes Grandma Kali," I said while smiling at her.

AT CARISSA'S HOUSE

Knock. Knock. Carissa opened the door.

"What it is?" Carissa asked.

"Nuthin much. What it do?" I replied.

Both of us laughed and then Carissa continued the conversation with the following question: "Girl, what's poppin with you?"

"Man, I'm pissed off! My sister got me in trouble again with her dumb butt. She make me sick. All she had to do was do what I told her to do."

"Girl, please. I wouldn't do what you told me to do either. Who are you? You ain't her momma," Carissa replied.

"So! Grandma told me that I was in charge and she wanted the house cleaned, so that means that everybody else that is younger than me need to listen including her," I replied.

"Forget about that, it's over and done with anyway."

"Yeah, Girl, you right. So what's up? What we getting into?" I asked.

"You know, time to take a journey," said Carissa.

"Ok, let's do it!"

Journey through the Neighborhood

Walking through the neighborhood, as we went to the "park," we heard the sounds of dogs barking, children laughing, and loud music playing.

"Well, well, well, look who else is on the playground," stated Carissa.

Before I could turn my head to see who else was on the playground, I was embraced by a handsome chocolate-colored gentleman with locks whose name was Daniel.

"What's up girl?" he said as he looked at me and smiled.

"Nothing much. What's up with you dude?" I replied.

"Man, nothing much. Y'all want to play basketball with us?" he asked.

"Doesn't matter to me. You know I love basketball." I replied as I laughed, turned to Carissa and said, "Do you want to play basketball Carissa?"

"Whatever y'all want to do is cool?" she agreed. With a loud voice I said, "It's on Daniel! We in! Y'all betta bring it!"

We played basketball for the next two hours. After the game ended, we noticed that our bright, blue, fluffy, white cloud-studded sky transitioned into a dark and gloomy, grey cloud-covered sky.

"Aw man! It's getting dark, guys. We have to go," I stated. Carissa nodded in agreement. We said goodbye to our friends and journeyed back to our places of residence.

Preparing for Next School Year: Time to Enter Middle School

Carissa and I power-walked through the neighborhood, in order to make it home before the street lights came on.

While walking home, we laughed as we talked about the events that took place on the basketball court. Then we each arrived at our homes. "I'm finally home," I thought to myself. Immediately, I went into the bathroom, ran some bath water, and took a relaxing bath while meditating on the fact that summer was almost over.

After my relaxing bath, I went into my bedroom and lay down in my bed. Soon, I went to sleep. For the remainder of the summer, Carissa, Korena, Daeon, Victoria, and other relatives and friends danced, laughed, sang, made things, and just spent time together. The summer was ending in two days. After the summer is over, I would be going to a new school: Blake Middle School.

As I arose the next morning, I remembered that soon the school year would be starting.

I thought to myself, "I can't go to middle school with these Canneridge gym shoes because I'm going to be fighting. The kids at my school already talk about me because I wear glasses. Man, these shoes will just add to the problem."

Based on my preconceived notion, I decided to ask Grandma Kali to purchase me some Mike gym shoes.

"Grandma Kali, can you buy me some Mike's?" I asked.

"No, what's wrong with the gym shoes you have?" she replied.

"I don't like them. Everybody at school wears Mike's."

"Canneridge is in my budget; therefore, if you want Mike's, then you need to figure out how to get yourself some Mike's. You betta do it the legal way, because if you go to jail, I'm goin to leave yo butt there. You know how to draw. Maybe you can sell your drawings. What else do you know how to do? Think about that and use it to make your own money," Grandma Kali replied.

After she said these things, Grandma Kali prepared to go to what she termed her favorite "charity": the Bingo Hall. When she pulled out of the driveway, I ran down the street to speak with Carissa.

Knock. Knock. Knock. "Who is it?" asked Carissa's mom.

"Tresa."

"Carissa, Tresa is here," she yelled.

Carissa opened the door. "What up lady?" she asked.

"Girl, I gotta tell you what my grandma just said."

"Hold on a second, I'm coming outside," replied Carissa.

She opened the door and came outside in her signature attire: a big T-shirt, baggy pants, and mismatched socks.

"Ha. Ha. Ha. Girl, what's wrong with you? I ain't going nowhere with you like that. You trippin," I said, as I laughed hysterically. She laughed as well.

Then she said, "What was it that you had to tell me?"

"I asked Grandma Kali for some Mike's and she basically told me to buy them myself," I replied while laughing. Carissa instantly laughed as well. Then she said, "Did she say how you supposed to that?"

"Yeah, she said to use what I already know how to do and start selling the things that I make. I thought that since we all know how to do things, we should create a girls club. At the girls club, we could draw pictures, make stuff and sell it to people in the hood. Once we earn enough money, we will buy everyone in the group some Mike's. What you think?" I asked.

"Sounds cool to me. Let's go see what Victoria thinks."

Much to our surprise, Victoria was already outside her home standing on the porch talking to Korena and April when we arrived.

"Hey y'all! I have an idea. Let's start a girls club. We would buy everyone in the group a pair of Mike's with the money that we earn from selling the items that we make. I'm going to draw pictures and sell them for approximately 25 cent to three dollars. What can each of you do?" I asked.

"I can hold on to our money and keep track of it," replied Victoria.

"I can make earrings, since Aunt Katie showed us how to make them," replied Korena.

"Me too!" April exclaimed.

"I forgot about that, April. I can make jewelry, design shirts and other clothing items too. Alright y'all, let's all ask our parents to purchase the stuff we need to create the items we will sale. Tomorrow when we meet, we will make the items, put prices on them, and start selling them by asking our parents and other folks on the block to purchase them. What do y'all think?" I asked.

"Yeah, let's do it!" everyone exclaimed.

After we made the decision to start the club, we switched topics, cracked jokes, danced in the driveway, and just enjoyed one another's company until it was approximately 9:00pm. Then we went home.

When Korena, April, and I arrived home, we ensured that things were back in place before Grandma Kali arrived. Much to our surprise, Grandma Kali arrived with Brown Castle burgers, candy bars, and a mystery bag.

"Here Tresa, this should get you started," she replied.

I looked into the bag, smiled and said, "Thank you".

Without us having to ask her, Grandma Kali had purchased markers, colored paper, plain paper, scissors, beads, glue sticks, bead string, t-shirts, hats, t-shirt iron-on paper, a glue gun and rhinestones.

The next day, each member of the girls club arrived at Victoria's house with all of our materials and worked from noon until approximately 6:00 pm, creating our products.

We went to the neighbors' houses close to each of our homes and asked them to purchase our creations.

After we sold all the items, we brought the money to Victoria's house, planned our next trip to the mall, decided to buy more materials and to purchase at least one of us some Mike's with the remaining balance.

Grandma Kali was so impressed with what we did with the items, that she informed us of the cost for each of the materials and took us to the store to purchase more materials using our money.

"It's y'all responsibility to make sure y'all purchase the materials for your business with your money," she replied. And then she took us home.

For the remainder of the summer we continued to have fun with one another and make money doing things that we loved to do. Who would have known that work could be this much fun!

CHAPTER 3

TRUTH REVEALED: FROM MIDDLE TO HIGH SCHOOL

New School

"What up doe girl? You ready?" I asked Carissa.

"Yeah, I'm good. Let's roll," stated Carissa, as she grabbed her backpack. Then we walked down the street.

During our walk, we dodged glass from the broken beer bottles that lay on the ground, while we did our best to avoid twisting our ankles as a result of improperly stepping on broken fragments of concrete within the sidewalk.

Walking around broken glass and being careful as we were stepping on broken fragmented sidewalks was like an annoying game of Hopscotch that we were forced to play daily.

While engaging in this annoying activity, Carissa made a suggestion regarding a destination that she wanted to visit before school: the penny candy store.

"Let's stop at the penny candy store on the way," she said.

"It's cool with me," I replied.

Expecting to see a huge sign with glaring lights announcing the presence of the penny candy store, I was presented with a much different image. It was located in an unlabeled white building. The windows and entrance door of the building had black bars installed across them.

We opened the door and rushed to stand in the single-file line located alongside of the glass cases within the penny candy store. These cases contained all sorts of delicious treats. In fact, our neighborhood penny candy store had it all: from candy to chips to cookies to ice cold drinks. Whatever you desired, you could find it there. The owner of the penny candy store was a woman by the name of Ms. Carey. Every time children entered her store, she greeted them with a smile and then offered them items that they recently purchased from her store.

It always amazed me that she knew exactly what each child liked to eat, especially considering the number of children who entered and exited her store on a regular basis.

Because this was my first time, she had to ask me what I desired; thus, I was the exception.

"Good morning ladies. How are you?" she asked.

"Fine," we both said to Ms. Carey.

"That's good. What would you like?"

As I looked at all of the glass cases containing the candy I desired, the thought of eating these treats made me feel as if I had gone to heaven.

With a huge smile I said, "I would like to get $2 worth of gummy worms, watermelon slices, and some cherry, grape, strawberry, apple, blue raspberry, and raspberry frooties, and some tootsie rolls, please."

"Well alright then, I love a young lady who knows what she wants," said Ms. Carey. Then she turned towards Carissa and asked, "And what would you like young lady?" "Well, I don't know . . . um . . . let me see," replied Carissa. Then the waiting game began.

Waiting on Carissa to make a decision was like waiting on eternity to pass over.

Finally, after approximately 5-10 minutes, Carissa decided to get some chips, a juice, and a few pieces of candy. After we acquired our goods, we exited the building and continued our path to Blake Middle School.

We arrived at the school about 10 minutes before the first bell rang. Blake Middle School was a large one story building with multi-colored hallways surrounded by hills of grass.

"See you later girl," Carissa yelled as she headed down the yellow hall.

"See you later," I yelled back as I looked at the map of the school, glanced over my class schedule, and then walked down the blue hall towards my first class.

"Is this room 120?" I asked.

"Yes it is, you may sit wherever you like," said Mrs. Belcher, my homeroom and language arts teacher.

Mrs. Belcher was a youthful looking, fair skinned, tall, slender lady with a short, feminine hair cut. She wore lots of jewelry and make up. In fact, her wedding ring was so large, that it always looked as though she was constantly pressing down a button using the middle finger on her left hand all day long.

Once the teacher had informed me that I could sit anywhere in the classroom and had pointed to the available seats, I entered the room and decided to sit in the first seat in the last row of the classroom. This seat was closest to the teacher's desk and there was at least one row of empty seats between me and the other students in the class.

After getting into arguments and fights with some of the students in previous classes at my old school, I knew that it would be best for me to sit alone. In fact, because it had become difficult for me to make new friends, I had gotten used to sitting in a seat away from everyone and not having many friends.

After a few weeks at my new school, once again I found myself involved in arguments with a few of the students. Although I continued to sit alone, much to my surprise, a girl decided to sit in the seat next to me and hold a conversation with me.

"You Tresa?" she asked. "Yeah, who are you?"

"I'm Missy. Hey, I heard that you were real mean. You don't seem mean to me," Missy said.

"I'm not real mean. I just don't like people. They make me sick. They always got something to say."

"Well, I don't always have something to say. Let's be friends," Missy said.

"That's cool wit me. So where you stay at?" I asked.

"On Sandisky."

"I stay on Sandisky too. I'mma come hang out at yo house for a minute after school one of these days. Is that cool wit you?" I asked.

"Yeah, that's cool," she replied.

"Ok, cool. Let's talk after class, because I can't get any bad grades, so I need to pay attention," I said while simultaneously laughing.

"Yeah me too," Missy said as she packed up her things in preparation for her transition to the next class upon the ring of the school bell.

At the sound of the bell, every kid in the room immediately darted out the door, as if they had seen a ghost and quickly attempted to flee from its presence.

"Get back in here! Now!" yelled Mrs. Belcher. Stunned, we returned to the classroom with our heads hanging low wondering, "Why is she calling us back into the classroom and she knows that we only have 10 minutes to make it to our next class?"

"Everybody sit back down. Don't ever leave my classroom before I properly dismiss you! Do you understand?" she asked the class.

"Yes," we responded.

Once the class was silent, she dismissed us. I walked as fast as I could and exited the classroom then traveled to my next class. Missy caught up with me in the hallway, pulled me to the side and said, "Girl, where you stay at for real?"

"On Sandisky. Where you stay at for real?" I replied.

She did not respond to my question. Instead she said, "Let's walk home together after school".

"That's cool with me. I'll meet you on top of the grass covered hill on the side of the school."

"Ok. Cool. I'll holla."

"Aight den," I replied, while exiting the classroom and traveling to my next class.

Throughout the remainder of the school day, I sat next to my new friend, Missy, in each classroom.

END OF SCHOOL DAY

As I traveled across the grass covered hill, I ran into my friend Carissa. "You ready?" she asked.

"Yeah, but I'm waiting on this girl named Missy who I met in class. She gone walk with us towards the house," I replied.

"Missy? Here you go picking up strays. Somebody new huh?" Carissa replied.

I laughed and responded, "She seems to be cool."

Shortly after I convinced Carissa of the character of Missy, Missy approached us along with another person I had never met.

"Missy, this is my friend Carissa. Carissa, this is Missy, my friend from class."

"Nice to meet you," they each replied.

"Y'all this is my friend Laheeta. Laheeta, this is my friend Tresa and her friend Carissa," Missy stated.

"Nice to meet y'all."

"Are we waiting on anyone else?" I asked.

"Naw, Let's go," Missy replied. We quickly departed in unity on the road to our destinations.

Four Months Later

Over the next four months, I became good friends with Missy's friend Laheeta.

Laheeta was a short dark-skinned young lady with short hair.

While on lunch break at school, Laheeta told me that her boyfriend was verbally abusive towards her. I told her that he better not ever say or do any of the things he did to her in my presence.

The next day, Missy and Laheeta were standing by the fence on the side of the school waiting for me.

As I approached them, I noticed that there was a tall, light-skinned guy with black hair standing by Laheeta. The closer I got to the group, the more upset I became; as I heard some of the most disrespectful words come out of the mouth of the light-skinned guy.

"That's why I don't like you no more!" He exclaimed. After yelling those words to her, he called

Laheeta a black female dog. In response, Laheeta cried fiercely and Missy cursed him out. Immediately, I rushed to her side and attempted to console her. However, my efforts to console her seemed to be ineffective.

It was at that moment two gates of opportunity were placed before me. Please review the descriptions of each gate and determine which gate you believe I chose to unlock and explore.

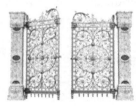 **Gate #1: Ignore him and console my friend who appeared to be hurt by what was said to her.**

By ignoring him and focusing on her, I could help my friend deal with her pain while simultaneously avoiding getting into any more trouble in my new school.

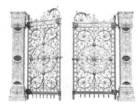 **Gate# 2: Demonstrate what I meant by the statement, "he better not say or do any of the things he did to you in my presence."**

By fighting him, I would be defending someone who I determined was unable to properly defend herself. At the same time, I would teach him a lesson about why it's important to treat people right.

What are the possible consequences presented by choosing each gate? Which gate would you choose and why? Which gate do you believe Tresa chose? What affect could the choice of each gate have on the relative(s) or guardian(s) of Tresa?

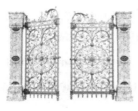 **Gate# 2: Demonstrate what I meant by the statement, "he better not say or do any of the things he did to you in my presence."**

By fighting him, I would be defending someone who I determined was unable to properly defend herself. At the same time, I would teach him a lesson about why it's important to treat people right.

While standing next to Laheeta, I became so enraged that instead of speaking up for her, I balled my fists into two tight circles of fire and stood in a boxing posture.

Swinging with my right fist, I punched him in the face. Then he tried to punch me; however, I deflected the punch and punched him again. We fought from the fence to the hill, to the middle of a busy street called Denaro Rd. and ended up inside the medical center located across the street from the school.

Finally, the fight came to an end inside of the medical center. While we were fighting, a crowd of people surrounding us yelled and laughed as if they were watching a tournament between their favorite players as they engaged in an all-out brawl.

Although many of the people were laughing, Laheeta was not. She yelled, "STOP!!!!! You're going to kill him!" Then she jumped in front of him.

I was so upset with her that I told her that this would be the first and the last time that I would ever defend her. The fight was over. However, over the next two weeks, Laheeta and I didn't speak to one another.

Meanwhile, Missy and I still visited one another and had fun together. During the school year, we gathered and partied on Saturdays.

One Saturday, I decided to walk down the street to Missy's house. As I walked down the street, I twirled my combination lock with my middle finger on my right hand and placed my keys in between the fingers on my other hand.

Suddenly, I was approached by a man named "Skillet". He grabbed my left wrist and said, "Hey gorgeous. My name is Skillet. What's your name?"

I yanked away from him and said, "Don't touch me! If you put your hands on me again, I will break them first then your face next. Then I will set you on fire." Laughing and smiling he replied, "Ooooo, I like 'em young and feisty. So tell me, pretty young thang, what's your name?"

"Leave me the hell alone or else!" I replied.

Immediately I gripped my keys, placed the ring of the lock around my middle finger, stood in a fighting stance, and looked at him fiercely, as if to say, "If you look or say something to me that I don't like, I will severely hurt you!"

"Alright little lady! I don't want no trouble, just thought that you were cute and wanted to holla at you. You need a real man. Not some lil boy. You need somebody who can take care of you, so when you ready, holla at a brotha," he replied as he walked away.

Thoroughly pissed off, I continued to walk to Missy's house. Upon arriving at Missy's home, I knocked on the door.

"Who is it?" asked Missy's mom. "It's Tresa," I replied.

Mrs. Johnson opened the door and gave me a big hug. "Hey Tresa! Come on in sweetie. Missy!"

"Huh?" yelled Missy.

"Tresa here," Mrs. Johnson replied.

"Tell her to come up here."

I walked past the living room and went up the stairs into Missy's bedroom.

"What's up girl?" Missy asked.

"Man, I'm pissed. Some old nasty punk grabbed me and tried to talk to me," I replied.

"What? Where? Who?" Missy asked as she stood with her eyes open wide apparently shocked by the details regarding what had happened to me.

"On the block past my house. Man, I can't believe that punk actually tried to talk to me and had the audacity to put his hands on me. I'm only twelve years old and he looked as if he was 27. Sicko! Ughhhh!" I replied.

"Man, that's messed up! I can't stand these nasty dogs in this hood! They make me sick! It's all good though," Missy replied.

"Girl, I promised to break his hands, face and set him on fire if he touched me again. I meant that thang. It's a good thing that he didn't touch me again because I was ready and I had this back pack on with my lighter and oil sheen in it." Missy laughed hysterically. This sparked a laughing frenzy engaged in by both Missy and me.

We continued to make fun of the situation. Surprisingly, I was no longer as upset as I was when I first arrived.

"I'm hungry. Are you hungry?" Missy asked.

"Yeah, I'm also thirsty."

"Well let's go down stairs and get something to eat," Missy said.

We darted downstairs towards the kitchen and noticed that no one else was in the home except for the two of us. While standing in the kitchen, Missy turned towards me and said, "I can make us some hamburgers. Do you want one?"

"Yes. Do you have some juice or some pop?" I replied.

"Yeah, go sit in the front room and I'll bring you some pop when I bring out the hamburgers," Missy replied.

"OK," I answered.

After about 20 minutes, Missy walked into the room with two plates which contained hamburger sandwiches and barbeque potato chips. She placed the plates onto the table then walked back into the kitchen to get our cups of pop. I was so thirsty, I grabbed my cup and placed it to my lips to drink; however, an unfamiliar smell hit my nostrils and caused me to stop.

"Girl, what's wrong with this pop?" I asked Missy.

"Ain't nothin wrong with your pop. I thought you said that you were thirsty. Girl, you trippin," Missy stated as she smirked.

"I am thirsty, but I ain't drinking this. This junk don't smell right!" I said. Missy laughed hysterically.

"What the heck is so funny? What did you do to my drink dude?" I asked.

"I thought I'd just spice it up for ya!" Missy said while still laughing.

"Girl, what's wrong with this pop?" I repeated while looking at her as if I were her mother demanding a response to my question.

"I mixed some of my dad's alcohol in it. I do it all the time for my drinks, especially if I've had a rough day. I thought I'd do the same for you. Dang! Can't surprise you with nothin!" she replied while still laughing.

I laughed and said, "What? You crazy! Girl, you know I don't drink. I can't believe that you tried to get a sista drunk. You don't need to be drinking no alcohol either. From here on out, I'll fix my own drinks or bring my own drinks. Thank you very much ma'am."

Both Missy and I laughed and continued to enjoy the day until it was time for me to return home. We continued this pattern throughout the week. However, on that Friday, I decided to go to Carissa's house to hang out with her.

When I arrived at Carissa's house, Carissa had already opened the door.

"It's finally Friday! What you gettin into lady?" I asked.

"Nothin much. Just chillin. What up doe?"

"Man, let's go to the mall." I suggested.

"Aight den, let's do it. What you gettin into Sunday morning?" she asked.

"Nothin. Sleep. What's up?"

"I want you to come to church with me," replied Carissa.

"That's cool. I'll go."

After this discussion, Carissa and I continued to have a great time. Finally, we went over Victoria's house to ask her if she wanted to go with us to the mall.

"Yes! Let's see if Korena and April want to go," replied Victoria.

After approximately two hours, we all met up at Carissa's house and walked down the street to stand at the Fantic Road bus stop to board the bus.

Once the bus arrived, we boarded it and enjoyed the company of one another as we journeyed to Stars Mall. Later, we all returned to our homes and went to bed.

"I wonder what Carissa's church is going to be like tomorrow," I pondered, as I turned out the lights and grasped the white, plush pillow located at the top of my bed and drifted to sleep.

JESUS

I arose from my bed at 7:30am and prepared for church.

"Where are you going?" Grandma Kali asked.
"I'm going to church with Carissa."

"Ok, see you later. As I ran towards the door, I realized that I didn't have my bible with me.

Immediately, I dashed up the stairs, grabbed it from off my dresser, departed through the front door and ran towards Carissa's house. After I arrived at Carissa's house, I knocked on the front door.

"Who is it?" Carissa replied.

"Tresa."

"What's up lady? I'll be ready in a moment. You can sit in here," Carissa said.

While sitting in her living room, I couldn't help but see all of the family pictures and ceramic décor. It reminded me of my house, because Grandma Kali had family pictures scattered in both the living and dining rooms.

Once she and her mom put on their coats, we left the house and traveled to The Land Baptist Church.

When we arrived at the church, we were greeted by a gentleman who was standing at the entrance.

"Good morning ladies," he stated.

Then he directed us to a classroom called Christian Academy specifically designed for our age group to study the bible. After Christian Academy, we went into the kitchen to eat snacks and fellowship with other members of the church before service. This was a shocking experience for me.

Although I had been to church with my Aunt Katie on several occasions, I couldn't remember a time in which the people at the church actually fed me before service. I enjoyed snack time because I was introduced to the Pastor, First Lady, other adults and their children prior to the start of the actual service. This was the first service I attended; however, after engaging in conversations with people during snack time, I felt as if I knew everyone. I felt like I was surrounded by family.

Sunday after Sunday, I repeated this pattern. Eventually, I accepted Jesus Christ as my Lord and Savior. Later on, I was baptized in the name of the Father, Son and Holy Spirit. Being reunited with God was a phenomenal experience that I would cherish for the rest of my life. On this particular Sunday, I returned home and went to sleep.

CHAPTER 4

NEW PEOPLE ON THE BLOCK

The next day, Carissa came to my house and knocked on the door. When I opened the door, she said, "What it do lady?"

"I'm good. What up doe?"

"I'm good. Have you met the new people on the block yet?" she replied.

"No. It's a whole bunch of them though," I responded.

"Yeah, I know right. Let's all go over there, introduce ourselves and say hi," Carissa suggested.

"That's cool wit me. I'll tell Korena and Victoria."

I rushed to tell Korena and Victoria. Afterwards, each of us gathered together at my house and crossed the wide road we called "an expressway" to meet the "new people." As we approached the house of the "new people," I thought to myself, "I wonder which of us is going to speak first?"

Immediately Carissa and I said, "Hello". After we spoke, Korena and Victoria also said "hello" to the new people.

Suddenly, the weird silence between the new people and my family and friends was broken like the connection between ice and an ice tray once force has been applied to the tray.

Once the silence was broken, we engaged in fun activities, such as racing one another and playing tag. For the following two months, we visited one another's homes, laughed and had lots of fun together.

The new peoples' names were Hattie, Lacey, Scott, Hunter, Dawn, and Castella.

Because of our ages, we easily became good friends with Hattie, Lacey and Scott, more so than with the other new people; however, their true colors quickly shined through after a few months.

For example, one day, while I was sitting on Hattie and Lacey's porch, both Hattie and Lacey said that they did not like Victoria. When I asked them for an explanation, Hattie and Lacey's response was that they didn't like her because, "she think she is all that". I asked Hattie and Lacey what they meant by the statement, "she think she is all that" and then sat quietly as they stated their reasons for not liking Victoria.

When the conversation switched to a discussion of how to violently attack Victoria, I could not remain silent any longer.

"We are going to kick her butt the next time we see her!" shouted Hattie and Laicey.

Upon hearing this threat, I stood up and responded, "Y'all ain't gone touch her. You betta gone head and talk to her and see if y'all can work it out, because ain't none of dat goin down. Period!"

"Oh it is, and whoever else jump in it they can get it too!"

"Well, I ain't bout to let no one touch her, so if you wanna bang, then we can throw down right here. We don't have to wait. What's up?" I replied.

After I made this statement, I stepped out of the center of both of them and stood in my fighting stance.

"Tresa, I thought we was cool? You gone take up for her? We not trynna fight you. Chill out," Hattie replied.

"Yep. I've known her longer and I'm not about to let nobody jump her. If y'all want to fight her, then you gone have to fight her one on one. I'm bout to go, so, I'll talk to y'all another day," I replied, as I stepped off the porch and crossed the street, arrived in front of my home and walked up the stairs towards my porch.

Recurring Nightmare: Truth Revealed

As I stood on the porch and pondered what I should do about this situation, two gates of opportunity were presented before me.

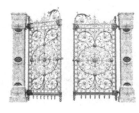 **Gate #1: Go tell Victoria what they said.**

Although this is considered instigation, I would be preventing my friend from being unaware of the fact that people who she considered to be her "friends" were planning to attack her.

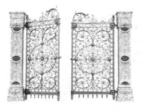 **Gate #2: Don't say anything to Victoria. Pretend as though everything was alright.**

By refusing to inform Victoria of what was said, I would be preventing myself from being an instigator. There is still a chance that our "friends" would not attempt to harm her.

Which gate do you believe would cause the greatest amount of harm to my relationship with Victoria? How would you address this situation? What are the potential advantages and disadvantages of each selection? Which gate do you believe I chose?

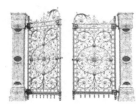 **Gate #1: Go tell Victoria what they said**

Although this is considered instigation, I would be preventing my friend from being unaware of the fact that people who she considered to be her "friends" were planning to attack her.

My pondering ended with the thought, "I gotta give Victoria the heads up about what these two chicks said."

Once I made the decision to tell Victoria, I bolted down the stairs of the porch and ran towards her house, up the stairs unto her porch and knocked on the door.

A tall dark-skinned man answered the door. It was Victoria's uncle. Upon opening the door, he said hello to me and yelled, "Victoria!"

"Huh?" she replied.

"Tresa here. Y'all go outside."

"Ok," she replied, as she walked down the stairs inside her home, out the front door and met up with me on her porch.

"What's up girl?" she asked.

"I just found out that our 'so-called' friends are fake!" I replied.

"What? Who?"

"Hattie and Lacey and nem. I was just over there and those chicks said that they didn't like you and they gone jump you. I told them that ain't nobody gone jump you, or else. Then I left their house," I replied.

"Those chicks know what's up! We not gone let those heiphas mess up our day. Girl let's see what Carissa is up to," said Victoria.

Before we could get down the last step on the porch, Carissa had arrived at Victoria's house.

"What's up girl?" we both asked Carissa.

"What it do?" she replied.

We laughed. Shortly after that, we told Carissa about Hattie and her sister. Carissa said, "Oh ain't nobody gone jump nobody. It ain't goin down like dat." We all laughed.

Within 15 minutes, Korena, Daeon, April, Johan, Chad, Tina, and Kathy joined us. Eventually, we brought out Victoria's radio, played our favorite songs, danced, cracked jokes, and laughed uncontrollably until it was time for all of us to return to our individual homes. Throughout the remainder of the summer we continued to get into verbal encounters with our 'so-called' friends.

Family Conflict

Although I was consistently engaged in verbal encounters with the new people, it was nothing compared to the fights I engaged in with my cousin Nolan.

Nolan was the brother of my first cousin on my father's side named Timina. Whenever I visited my dad, he would take us over their house to see their mother: Aunt Cammie.

Aunt Cammie was the mother of Nolan, Timina, Cam, Ken, Jeff and Semiah. If Nolan, Timina, my other cousins and I were left alone in the home for a period of time, Nolan would shout the following phrase towards me: "That's why your dad is gay!" At those moments, I felt as if my dad must be defended, since he was not present to defend himself. I also believed that it was impossible for my dad to be 'gay' so I didn't understand why Nolan would call him 'gay'.

When I was a child, whenever someone used the word 'gay' to describe a male, it meant that the male he or she was referring to only liked men, so they would only be in a relationship with a man.

As I grew older, I realized that the proper term to use would have been homosexual in that case, especially since the word 'gay' actually means merry or having a lively mood.

People who operate under a different sexuality are not always happy, so the usage of the word 'gay' was inappropriate. Also, I didn't believe that someone could be interested in both men and women, so I didn't believe that bisexuality was what Nolan was referring to when he blurted out, "That's why your dad is gay!"

Surely, my father was not homosexual. After all, he was the father of my sister, brother and I. He never told me that he was homosexual. My father did not keep secrets from me.

Because my dad and I were very close, I knew that if it were true that he was interested in both men and women, I would have been the first to know.

As a result of my beliefs with regards to my dad's sexuality and our relationship, the disrespect exhibited by Nolan enraged me every time it happened. Nolan had to learn how to respect my father. I decided that I was the right person to show Nolan how to respect my dad. I would defend my father at all costs. After all, Nolan had the audacity to call my dad, 'Ruby' as if to add salt to the injury he placed on my heart by disrespecting my dad.

In light of the behaviors exhibited by Nolan and myself, one day in particular comes to mind.

On that day, I was over Aunt Cammie's house laughing and enjoying spending time with my cousin Timina. Shortly afterwards, my dad, Aunt Cammie, and the other adults left to go get a few things from the store. Once Nolan noticed that they were gone, he started saying rude things to me such as, "That's why you ugly! Nobody likes you! etc."

"Nolan, you betta stop. You already know how she is. Leave her alone!" Timina shouted towards her brother. Timina consistently did her best to stop us from fighting; however, I was determined that this would be the last day that Nolan would disrespect me or my father.

While Nolan was in the middle of making his next rude remark, I quietly walked from the front room were the both of us were standing into the kitchen.

Once I entered the kitchen, I gathered steak knives in both of my hands, as an attempt to let him know that danger was on the rise. You would have thought that he would have stopped dead in his tracks with regards to completing his statement, but that was not the case.

After about five minutes, he yelled his favorite set of taunting words: "That's why your daddy is gay!"

I was so enraged that I could not respond to his remarks with words. I felt my hands heat up, as if they were placed inside of a furnace. I could no longer see him. Everything I saw was red! Immediately, I aimed and threw the steak knives at his head and heart.

Nolan bolted out of the house. I chased him for three blocks throwing steak knives at him. As he ran in an "S-shaped" pattern, each knife missed him by no more than one inch. Timina was screaming for me to stop.

Although she and I were very close, I couldn't stop myself. I was determined to kill him. I felt that he totally disrespected my father for the last time. Enough was enough.

After Nolan was no longer in my sight, I finally calmed down. At that moment, I stopped chasing him and traveled back to the house; while feverishly collecting the thrown knives in order to wash them and put them back in the kitchen.

Later, Nolan, my dad and Aunt Cammie arrived home at the same time. Nolan did not come near me. We did not tell my dad or aunt about the events that occurred during their time away. Instead, Timina and I talked about everything that happened.

As a result of our discussion, I decided to drop the issue and go to sleep. When I arose the next morning, it was time to return home. Both my brother and I said good-bye to my Aunt Cammie, gave everyone a hug, and traveled with Grandma Kali back home.

IDENTITY REVEALED

Home sweet home! The thought of climbing into my bed and snuggling with my favorite pillow consumed me as I bolted up the stairs to my bedroom. I put on my pajamas, got into my bed and drifted to sleep.

"You can't get me! You can't get me!" Timina, Nolan, Delane, Mia, other cousins and I all yelled as a man with a blank face grabbed us one by one and threw us onto the bed.

Laughing hysterically, we did not hear him the first time when he told us that he was tired and wanted everyone to leave the room and go downstairs, but the second time he said it, we all responded.

Like wild oxen, we stampeded out of the room, but I was caught in the grasp of the one who caused the stampede: the blank faced man.

"Tresa, you can stay in here with me," declared the blank-faced man. Then he placed me onto his bed. "Did you know that you are my favorite niece?"

"No," I replied.

"Well, you are and you are so beautiful. Your mother was just as beautiful as you are," declared the blank-faced man. I smiled.

Then he asked me to come closer to him. As an obedient child, I honored his request. After getting closer to the blank-faced man, I could smell a horrible stench protruding from his mouth and through his skin; it was as if someone took all the liquor and wine available in the country and poured it down his throat.

"Do you want to play another game?" Excited by the thought of continuing to have fun, I exclaimed, "Yes!"

"Let's play house. I'm the father and you're the mother. Now lie down," he said.

I lay down on the bed. Immediately, the blank-faced man positioned himself on top of me. He kissed me on my face and neck. Then he put one of his hands on my butt and placed the other hand into my pants and lifted my panties while I laid there trying not to throw up, yet so terrified that I couldn't yell. Then the blank-faced man looked into my eyes.

Suddenly, he acted as if he had seen a ghost and jumped off of me. At that moment, I awoke and thought to myself, "I'm tired of waking up from the same nightmare. When will it stop?"

Sweating, shivering, and still sleepy, I arose, gripped my baby doll and thought about the nightmare. Quickly, I noticed that all the lights were out.

I was so afraid of the dark that I walked to the bathroom and turned on the lights. I looked into the mirror and said to myself, "I must know who this is. I am tired of having the same dream. I will no longer be afraid. When I find out who this is, I am going to kill him because of what he did to me." Afterwards, I went back to my bedroom and went to sleep again.

This dream repeated itself, but finally one time I could distinctively see the facial features of the blank-faced man. To my surprise, I knew him very well. His name was Uncle Roland.

Uncle Roland was always playing with the children. He was the "fun" uncle. I was infuriated at my discovery that he was the culprit of the abuse I had experienced.

After rising from my bed, I got dressed and traveled to school. While at school, I cursed out whoever decided to say something rude to me or failed to do what I told them to do. At times, I shouted the phrase: "LEAVE ME ALONE!" to other children who talked to me at school. I didn't want to talk to anyone. All day long I thought to myself, "How dare he do this to me? He must don't know my daddy like he think he does! He gone get his! I'm telling my daddy and my grandma!"

After school ended, I finally had an opportunity to have some fun with my friends, as we walked home from school. The ground was covered with snow. People were laughing and having a great time. Children were throwing snow balls at one another.

It was what most people would consider to be a great winter day, but the great winter day turned sour after I was hit with one of the snowballs that was thrown. I was furious!

"Who threw that snowball?" I demanded. My friends looked around to see who threw it. Then they said, "Colby threw it. You may not want to mess with him though."

Colby was an extremely tall kid who always had people following him; especially the girls in the school. Many of the girls considered him to be attractive.

Standing next to Colby was like standing next to the GM building located in downtown Detroit, with regards to the height and weight differential between he and I. However, those facts did not matter to me. All I wanted was for people to leave me alone.

Although I didn't know him and he didn't know me, I turned towards my friends and said, "I ain't scared of him! He bet not hit me with another snowball, I know that much!" They laughed.

SMACK! I was hit with another snowball. By this time, I was thoroughly pissed. I wanted to throw a brick at his head, but there weren't any loose bricks near me. Realizing that I was carrying my boots in a bag, I yelled,

"Whoever threw that snowball, if you hit me with another snowball, I'm going to crack you in yo head with these boots! Watch what you are doing! Stop throwing snowballs!"

SMACK! I got hit again. That was the last straw. I dashed through the crowd clutching my bag of steel-toed Notice Me boots in my hand, then leaped as if I was about to dunk a basketball through the rim and hit him in the head three times before landing on my feet. I hit him so hard that one of the boots flew out of my bag into the middle of the street. At that moment, the fight began. I stood in my stance. My head was at his stomach. I jumped up and punched him in the jaw. He punched me. I jumped up and punched him again; however, this time when he punched me, I fell on the ground. As he was walking away, I got back up and cursed him out. One of the girls who really liked him came up to me grinning and said, "You all right."

"Get out of my face before I kick yo butt!"

"It ain't ova boy!" I yelled. My friends were shocked. They kept saying, "Girl, I can't believe you hit him. I can't believe you got that many hits in. That's crazy! He be beaten dudes down!"

The rest of their comments were like a vapor, I could see them talking, but I wasn't paying much attention because I was still furious.

Approximately 15 minutes later, Colby approached me, but not close enough for me to hit him.

He said, "I apologize for hitting you like that, especially since you are a girl. My bad."

"Whateva, I'm still gone knock yo butt out! It ain't ova boy! You betta get away from me!" I yelled. Colby walked away shaking his head. All of us dispersed and went to our homes.

After I arrived home, I noticed that my lip was hurting. I looked at it in the mirror to see what was going on with my lip. To my surprise, it was busted.

No one ever had gotten that close to me during a fight. I thought to myself, "WHAT!!! DO I SEE BLOOD?"

Because my lip was bleeding, I called my dad and told him what happened. My dad said that he was going to see if he could get a ride to come over to my grandma's house so that I could point out Colby.

"I'm going to find him and kill him!" I screamed.

"Calm down Tresa. I'm doing my best to get there. I'll call you back in a few minutes," he said. I hung up the phone.

At this moment I was presented with two gates that led to different lives.

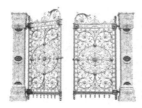 **Gate #1: Take my dad's advice. Do things that typically calmed me down, such as read a good book, put on some jazz music, take a long bath etc.**

By taking my dad's advice, I would be saving two lives: Colby's life (by not killing him) and my life (by preventing myself from going to jail for premeditated murder, which meant a sentence of at least 25 to life in prison). I would also be exercising control over the anger that I felt instead of allowing it to control me.

 **Gate #2: Allow my anger to turn into rage and search the neighborhood for Colby to do exactly what I said: "Kill him!"**

If I allowed my anger to turn into rage and search for Colby for the purpose of killing him, I would be showing everyone in the neighborhood that I'm not someone they want to mess with. I would be showing them that I do what I say I will do. I also would be ensuring that Colby would never be able to make me that mad again, because he would no longer be alive to do so. Then everyone else in the neighborhood would just leave me alone and I would have peace.

Which gate would you choose to walk through and why? Which gate do you believe I actually chose? Which gate do you believe I should have chosen and why? Can you think of any different methods that someone can use to calm down if they were very angry? Please describe the different methods and why you believe they would work.

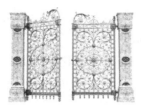 **Gate #2: Allow my anger to turn into rage and search the neighborhood for Colby to do exactly what I said: "Kill him!"**

If I allowed my anger to turn into rage and search for Colby for the purpose of killing him, I would be showing everyone in the neighborhood that I'm not someone they want to mess with. I would be showing them that I do what I say I will do. I also would be ensuring that Colby would never be able to make me that mad again, because he would no longer be alive to do so. Then everyone else in the neighborhood would just leave me alone and I would have peace.

I bolted down the stairs. Enraged by the events that occurred, I dashed into the kitchen, grabbed two butcher knives, and stormed out the side door of the house.

As I marched down the driveway, I put the butcher knives together in one hand, and put on one of my winter gloves. I alternated the location of the butcher knives and put on the other winter glove. After putting on my gloves, I placed a butcher knife in each hand and walked the neighborhood searching for Colby. Once I turned the corner, I saw a group of guys wrestling in the snow.

"A yo, y'all seen Colby?" I asked. "Nah, we ain't seen him."

"Aight den. Thanks," I replied.

As I continued to parade through the streets searching for Colby for about an hour, suddenly, I glanced at my watch. I couldn't believe that it was 4:00pm and I still had not located Colby. Because Grandma Kali was always home by 5:00pm, I needed to hurry up and get home. In order to avoid getting into more trouble, I sprinted to the house and arrived home before Grandma Kali.

I ran up the driveway, went into the side door, and placed the butcher knives back in the cutting block that I had taken them from. Then, I went upstairs, shut the door, worked on my homework, and listened to my favorite rapper's song, "Me Against the World," by Tupac Shakur.

Whenever I listened to this song in the midst of an episode of rage, I typically calmed down. The lyrics were so poetically written that I felt as if Tupac was the only person who really understood me.

Many times in my life, I felt as if I was against the world. I felt as if no one was alive and willing to help me. My mom was dead and it seemed as if everyone I had gotten close to kept dying and left me here in "hell on earth". I wanted to die too. I was not afraid of dying. Whenever I allowed anger and rage to overtake me, Grandma Kali would say, "If you don't control that anger, you gone end up dead or in jail." Sometimes I would say, "I want to die". To me, death meant that I could finally be with my mom, older cousin, great aunt and others who had died.

I believed they had an easy life because they no longer had to be in this struggle called "life" and deal with people constantly doing or saying things to disturb their peace. I desired peace, but rage convinced me that the only way to get it was to kill or injure those who disturbed it.

These thoughts were interrupted with a single command from Grandma Kali, "Tresa! Turn that music down!" she exclaimed.

I turned the music off and came downstairs. "Hi Grandma, I'm finished with my homework. Can I go down to Carissa's house?"

"Yea," she replied. I put on my winter coat and accessories, stepped out the door and traveled to Carissa's house.

Once I arrived at Carissa's house, I knocked on the door and Carissa answered the door.

"Who is it?"

"Tresa," I replied. Carissa opened the door, grabbed her winter coat and other items then came outside.

"What up doe?" I asked. "What it is," she replied.

Then, I told her about the altercation I had at school.

After we laughed and talked about what happened, I shared with her what my uncle did to me. She was highly upset.

Much to my surprise, Carissa revealed to me that she had experienced something similar. We talked about telling our parents and we agreed to do so. After we laughed and wrestled with a few guys in the neighborhood, we returned to our homes.

As I entered the house, I shouted "Grandma!" and looked around the front room to see where she was. "What?" she answered.

I heard her voice blaring from the top of the stairs, so I ran up the stairs and told Grandma Kali that I really needed to talk to her.

Immediately, I told her what Uncle Roland had done to me. She appeared to be disturbed by this information. I thought to myself, "She is going to make sure that he doesn't get away with this. He will know not to put his filthy hands on anybody else in my family!"

Much to my surprise, Grandma Kali said, "Why didn't you tell me this when it happened? It's too late now. There's nothing I can do about it."

I felt as if someone had deflated my hot air balloon. I felt hurt and confused. I was thirteen years old. I thought to myself, "How could it be too late?"

At that moment, I decided that, since Grandma Kali couldn't do anything about it, I would tell my dad. I believed that once I told my dad what happened to me, he would make sure that Uncle Roland paid for his reckless behavior. I thought to myself, "My dad has always defended me. He has cursed people out for simply speaking to me in an inappropriate manner. I've seen him consistently beat up Uncle Kent for minor offenses. This was major! That's it! Since it is the weekend, I know that my brother and I are going over my dad's house. I will tell him this weekend."

"Tell All" Weekend

After we arrived at my dad's house, I was greeted by my cousin.

"What up cuz?" asked Timina.

"Nuthin much. What up doe T?" I asked, as I smiled and embraced my cousin. We laughed, joked around, and just had fun until it became very late in the evening.

During the evening, I pulled my dad to the side and told him what Uncle Roland had done to me. His face looked as if he was deeply troubled. "I'll take care of it," he replied in a stern voice.

I trusted that my dad would handle this situation. For a moment, I left it alone. However, later I was informed by Uncle Kent that my dad didn't believe me. After hearing those words, I was devastated! I looked up to my dad. If nobody else would defend me, I knew that he would. Hurt, but masking it with anger, I decided to take matters into my own hands. I thought to myself, "I will kill him myself! Then he will never be able to hurt anyone else. Man, it's going down tomorrow night!" Furious, emotionally drained and sleepy, I closed my eyes and went to sleep.

The next day, I arose, determined to enjoy the festivities of the day. I refused to think about what Uncle Kent said regarding my dad's feelings about what happened to me.

Nevertheless, it was very difficult not to think about it. My communication with my dad had changed. Before this new information, I laughed with my dad and enjoyed being around him.

Now, after receiving this disturbing information, I found myself avoiding being in his presence.

I was angry! Forgiveness was a thought that I felt as though I could not entertain. I believed that justice had to be served. I was both the prosecutor and the judge.

My verdict for Uncle Roland's actions was death at the hands of the victim: me.

Throughout the day, everyone was having a great time; however, early in the morning everyone went to sleep, except me.

Because of my determination to "right" a "wrong", I pretended to be asleep and later rose to execute judgment. I tiptoed past everyone and went into the kitchen. Quickly, I grabbed the sharpest and largest knife I could find. As I crossed the threshold that separated the kitchen from the living room, I traveled down the hallway and went into the room where Uncle Roland slept. I positioned myself and placed the knife close to his throat.

At that moment, I heard a male voice say, "Thou Shalt Not Kill." I looked around to see where that voice came from but I couldn't see anyone. I tried to cut his throat again. The same voice spoke to me in a louder tone saying, "THOU SHALT NOT KILL!" This startled me.

Although I had read biblical scriptures for years, I never heard a voice quote the scriptures that I knew. The voice sounded like that of a man. I was a female and my mouth was closed when I heard this sound; surely, it was not my voice. There wasn't anyone else visibly present at the time that I heard this voice. I was frustrated! My purpose was to execute judgment upon someone who had offended me, but I felt as though I was not allowed.

Discouraged, I thought to myself, "Ok, not tonight, but tomorrow it is on," as I tiptoed out of the room, down the hall, and into the kitchen.

I placed the knife where it was previously positioned and returned to my resting place for the weekend. This pattern of attempting to kill Uncle Roland occurred for about three months.

During that time, I continued to hear the same voice each time I made my attempt to execute "my judgment" upon Uncle Roland.

Finally, I decided that killing him wasn't worth it. I ceased this activity, but I told Uncle Roland that I knew what he did to me, and if I ever heard that he did it to someone else or worst, I would kill him.

Although it appeared as if he did not believe me, I meant every word. Over a period of time, I asked many of my female cousins if he had ever touched them.

To my surprise, he had not. Later, I realized that the voice I heard was the voice of God himself. I thank God for saving two lives with one phrase. Had I executed my judgment upon Uncle Roland, I would have been in jail and he would have been dead. Neither one of us would have accomplished God's purpose for our lives because of one act of rage.

Conflicting Messages

The next day, my brother and I arose to go home. We packed all of our things and waited for Grandma Kali to arrive. After she arrived, we traveled with her home. Upon entering the house, I was so exhausted that I went straight upstairs into my bedroom and went to sleep.

The sleep that I experienced on that night was unlike any other sleep. I didn't wake up in the middle of the night and dash into the bathroom to wipe the sweat off of me. The previous recurring nightmare did not even trickle across my mind. I slept peacefully. What a wonderful feeling! I arose the next morning, charged and ready for school.

While getting ready for school, this thought came into my mind, "You asked everybody else except for one of the closest people to you: your sister."

I had to know if he had done the same thing to her, so I asked my sister if she had experienced it. "No," she replied. I felt relieved while simultaneously feeling upset.

"Why did he do that to me? At one point in my life, he was one of my favorite uncles because he would play games with us. How could he do such a thing? How could God let him do that to me?" I thought to myself, while my sister and I walked to school.

Once we arrived at school, we dispersed like steam pushing through the lid of a boiler as we walked through the crowds in the hallway and went into our separate classrooms.

While in each of my classes, I took notes as fast as possible in order to ensure that I didn't miss anything. When school ended, I walked home with my friends, and my sister walked home with her friends. Rarely did we walk home together, so we typically arrived at the house at separate times.

Once I arrived home, I went into the dining room table and completed my homework. The words that I did not understand, I put on a separate sheet of paper. I decided that when Grandma Kali arrived, I would ask her what those words meant.

After I had placed four words onto my separate sheet of paper, I heard a sound at the front door. Someone was attempting to use their keys to enter the house. Suddenly, the door opened. As I suspected, it was none other than Grandma Kali.

I waited for approximately 30 minutes before springing my questions on her.

"Grandma Kali, how do you spell 'exquisite' ?" I asked.

"Look it up."

"But I don't know how to spell it. How am I going to look it up?" I asked, while being annoyed that she wouldn't just spell the word for me.

"Sound it out, and then look in the dictionary for the word. After you find it, tell me the spelling and what the word means."

I thought to myself, "More work? Girl, why did you ask her? Now you have more homework." I just wanted to put an intelligent word on my homework paper to try to stand out. I'd heard people use it before.

Nevertheless, I sounded out the word, looked it up in the dictionary, wrote down the definition, and shared it with Grandma Kali in an attempt to appease her.

However, the next few words out of her mouth were, "Now study this definition and the spelling so you will know how to spell the word and what it means next time I ask you about it."

When I heard that response, I thought to myself again, "Aw, man, more work?" After running into this same scenario over the week, I realized that I enjoyed looking up words and learning what they meant. I had new words to add to my vocal arsenal. I said to myself, "Maybe I can use some of these words this weekend." However, that idea quickly vanished as I thought about going over my dad's house and how we typically interacted as a family over there.

Yes! The weekend was finally here. My brother and I had already packed our bags. As soon as Grandma

Kali said that she was ready to go, we would have to place our bags into the car.

"Let's go Tresa and Daeon!" she exclaimed.

Upon hearing the phrase "Let's Go," we bolted down the stairs with our bags in hand, placed them into the trunk, entered the car and traveled to our dad's new house.

WEEKEND OF SURPRISES

"Bye Grandma!" We exclaimed, as we swiftly opened the doors to the vehicle and raced to the top of the stairs to go inside our dad's new house on Cecrest Street.

"We are about to go over your Aunt Cammie's house, so put y'all stuff up and let's go," my dad instructed as we entered his house. We followed our dad's instructions, and then we got into his car and traveled to Aunt Cammie's house.

As we entered Aunt Cammie's house, I noticed that smoke filled the air as relatives told jokes, laughed, and drank their alcoholic beverages. While the adults had a good time, the children all went outside and raced one another.

We also wrestled and simply enjoyed each other's company, until we were rudely interrupted by a typical occurrence: a family fight.

Unfortunately, it was not unusual for someone to have had too much to drink and as a result, start a fight with someone else in the home.

Each weekend, different people engaged in physical altercations with the exception of two: my dad and Uncle Kent. There was rarely an occasion that they did not fight one another.

In fact, Uncle Kent and my dad would argue all the time, but things would intensify if Uncle Kent or my dad had one too many drinks. This was one of those occasions.

All the children were outside playing, when my dad and Uncle Kent came out of the house arguing. In the middle of the argument, my dad punched Uncle Kent so hard that he knocked out two of his teeth. Uncle Kent tried to defend himself, but his attempts were unsuccessful.

I was so used to seeing fights occur, that I was not shocked by this display of aggression. To me, my dad was simply defending himself. I thought that Uncle

Kent must have said or did something to deserve the brutal treatment he received.

After the fight, as usual, Uncle Kent pulled me to the side and said, "Talk to your father. He ain't gone keep doing this to me. I ain't no punchin bag."

Although I felt bad for Uncle Kent, I also knew that, because I was a kid, there wasn't anything that I could do. I couldn't stop my dad from attacking him, just as I couldn't stop Uncle Kent from antagonizing my dad; thereby, provoking the supposedly "unwanted" aggression.

I was also taught that, for every action there is a reaction; thus, if someone doesn't like the reactions they are getting, they should change their actions.

In this case, whether that meant to totally discontinue being close friends and brothers, make an effort to discontinue excessive consumption of alcoholic beverages, or cease agitating behaviors; the decision rested with Uncle Kent and not me. Therefore, I refused to say anything to my dad about the fight, unless he opened the door for discussion.

After things became calm again, people laughed and enjoyed one another's company until everyone dispersed to their homes to get some rest.

The next day we arose and prepared ourselves for new experiences.

This day started with my brother and me going into the basement to play with our dog, Tango.

Although his face was about the size of a basketball, I believed that Tango was a very friendly Rottweiler. At least he was friendly to me and my brother.

While in the basement, we threw things towards Tango so that he could dash to retrieve the items and give them back to us. It was so much fun. He was so quick and smart. I loved my dog!

Even though I was only able to spend time with Tango on the weekends, it was worth it.

"Tresa and Daeon, come on. It's time to go," my dad said.

We ran up the stairs, exited the front door, and met with my dad on the porch. As usual, it was time to go visit our relatives.

As my brother and I entered the vehicle, I thought to myself, "I hope we can all just have a good time today without any fights or arguments, but we'll see." My thoughts were interrupted each time we arrived at a different relatives' house.

We had a great time at each of our relatives' houses. The wonderful thing about that day was that no one argued or fought. Everyone had a great time! Afterwards, we all returned to our homes.

Upon entering my dad's house, my brother and I hung our coats up, put on our pajamas, and we lay down on the couch.

After a day of running, laughing and playing, we drifted to sleep quickly.

In the midnight hour, I arose to use the bathroom. I eased off the couch, turned left, and proceeded to enter the bathroom; however, I was startled at the noise that came from my dad's bedroom.

I looked in the direction of the bedroom. I noticed that the door was partially opened. As I looked through the opening, I saw something that disgusted me and caused me to be angry all at the same time.

I saw my dad having sex with Uncle Kent. Uncle Kent was bent over the bed while my dad was placing his penis into what looked like Uncle Kent's behind. I was devastated!

Quickly, I turned around and went towards the basement door. As I cried vehemently thinking to myself, "How could this be? I'm such an idiot! I've been fighting my cousin Nolan all this time for calling my dad 'gay'. I thought that he was disrespecting my dad and lying, when all along, he was telling the truth! How could my dad be homosexual and have three children? Why didn't he tell me? Why didn't anyone else tell me? Did my mom ever know?"

So many questions bombarded my mind. Hurt and distraught, I opened the door to the basement and tiptoed down the stairs to be with one of my best friends: Tango. Surprisingly, Tango did not bark at all.

I wiped tears from my eyes with my left hand and held Tango close to me with my right hand. "Tango, you are the only one who has never let me down. I can trust you, if I can't trust anybody else," I whispered to him.

In response, he attempted to lick my face, but I moved my face away from his mouth and allowed him to lick my hand.

After a few minutes of silent whimpering, I decided to avoid the possibility of seeing the same sight that I had just seen.

Instead of going upstairs to go and try to use the bathroom again, I decided, "I don't have to use it that bad. I can hold it." Then I returned to my resting place upstairs and went to sleep.

CHAPTER 5

TRANSITION TO GREATNESS: FROM HIGH SCHOOL TO COLLEGE AND BEYOND

HIGH SCHOOL GRADUATION

The next morning, I arose and prepared for the day as if nothing had happened the night before. Although I was still hurt and upset, he was still my dad and I loved him. I decided to enjoy the events of the day until it was time for my brother and me to return to Grandma Kali's house.

After we returned home to Grandma Kali's house, we took baths and put on our pajamas. I couldn't seem to get myself to stop thinking about what I saw this past weekend. It grossed me out! I was still shocked. With all these new findings, I didn't feel like starting a new school tomorrow; but I knew that it was inevitable.

"Starlight High School here I come," I sighed as I rested upon my bed and drifted to sleep.

First day of High School

Ring! Ring! Ring! Was the sound that I heard at 5:00 am. In an attempt to relieve myself of the experience of this annoying sound, I reached over to the dancing alarm clock, used the bottom half of my balled fist, and pounded the alarm clock until it was finally silent.

"Tresa! Get Up!" exclaimed Grandma Kali. I remained in my position for about five minutes. Then, I jumped out of the bed and prepared for school.

Nervous, yet confident, I thought about the fact that today would be the first day that I would ride in a bus to school. In fact, I would have to take multiple buses to get to school on time.

Although Maxine High School was located in my neighborhood, I wanted a change of venue. Not to mention the fact that I had passed the admissions exam necessary to go to Starlight High School.

This exam allowed me to be placed in the advanced college preparation educational program, titled Center for International Studies and Commerce (CISC), located within Starlight High School.

At approximately 5:45 am, Grandma Kali and I left the house and traveled to the Fantic Road bus stop.

Once the bus pulled up, Grandma Kali told me that she would see me later and I boarded the bus to travel to school.

After arriving at school, I stood in line and waited to enter the building. While standing in line, I thought to myself, "This school looks nice. I hope it makes a difference in my life; but we will see."

I believed that by going to this school, I would finally be able to have peace. Surely, I would not have any altercations at the new school. After all, I've heard that these students are nerds. Nerds don't pick on people or try to start fights over stupid stuff. I soon discovered that these thoughts were a poor representation of reality.

After the first four classes had passed, I carried my books in my hand and walked to my next class.

However, my path to class was interrupted by a senior student who had pushed me and knocked all of my books out of my hand.

As the books hit the ground, the culprit and a friend of hers laughed. "Next time, move out my way freshman!" she replied.

At that moment, I was presented with two gates to choose from. Each led to a different type of life.

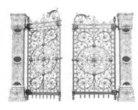 **Gate #1: Pick up my books and tell an adult about what happened.**

By choosing this option, I could get to class on time, while simultaneously ensuring that something was done to the young lady who knocked down my books. Although some classmates may laugh at me, at least I wouldn't entertain the spirit of rage; thereby, potentially causing more harm to me and others involved.

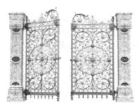 **Gate #2: Force her to pick up my books; thereby, teaching her a lesson about bullying.**

By choosing this option, I would be able to teach her a lesson regarding why she shouldn't bully freshman students. I would also be ensuring that no one else would attempt to bully me. The purpose of this action would be to restore the peace that I was experiencing at my new school.

Which choice would you choose and why? Which choice do you think I chose? Are there any other potential options that I could have considered in order to solve this problem? After you have answered these questions, turn to the next page to see what choice I chose and how opening that gate affected my life. See you on the other side of the gate.

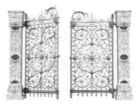 **Gate #2: Force her to pick up my books; thereby, teaching her a lesson about bullying.**

By choosing this option, I would be able to teach her a lesson regarding why she shouldn't bully freshman students. I would also be ensuring that no one else would attempt to bully me. The purpose of this action would be to restore the peace that I was experiencing at my new school.

"PICK MY BOOKS UP, NOW!" I exclaimed, while glaring at this girl who appeared to be at least two inches taller than me. "Who do you think you talking to, freshman?" In response to this question, I pushed her into the window on the second floor of the school. Once the window flew open, I grabbed her to make sure that she didn't fall out the window. "I should drop you right out this window for being stupid. You gone pick my books up or you goin out the window! What you gone do?" I said to her with a stern voice and a smile on my face.

She looked petrified! She started to speak, but couldn't seem to get the words to flow out of her mouth.

While I was holding her out of the window, a friend of mine shouted, "Hey, what's up? What's going on?" he asked.

"She knocked my books down on purpose and she about to pick them up or get thrown out this window," I said to him, while laughing.

"Man, come on! I'll pick up your books. It ain't that serious! Just let her go," he said.

"Naw man, you don't have to do dat. She gone do it. She is the one who knocked my books down, not you." He did not listen. He picked up my books and continued to ask me to pull her back in the window and release her.

After seeing my books in his hand, I pulled her back in the window and grabbed my books from him. The girl and her friend both ran down the stairs.

"Hey, I see somebody still got issues from middle school," he said, as he smiled and looked at me.

We laughed and went our separate ways; however, we arrived at the same destination: English class.

Class was great! I learned so many new things and my teacher seemed to be very nice. Her name was Ms. Chaney. She was tall, dark-skinned with salt and pepper-colored short hair.

During class, she said things that caused us to laugh. She was able to control the class without making it void of joy in the process.

Over the course of the next seven months, I had grown to love her, as if she were a member of my family. Each day that I went to school, I was excited about being able to help Ms. Chaney do things in class.

I loved the fact that I could talk to her about anything.

One day, I shared with her one of the greatest emotional pains that I continuously experienced whenever I thought about my mother. I shared with her how I missed her. I also told her that at the age of seven, I was told that my mother had died of pneumonia.

At that moment, I couldn't stop crying. Ms. Chaney showed such empathy and compassion that all the question marks regarding whether or not she truly cared about me were answered in that moment. I went to her office after class to talk to her sometimes and she listened to me. She also allowed me to cry on her shoulder whenever I needed to. She was one of the best teachers I had ever encountered.

From that day forward, I arose excited about going to school. One morning on a cold rainy day, I walked to the bus stop by myself and a stray dog followed me. I used to play with this stray dog all the time in the neighborhood. On this day, it waited with me for a short period of time then departed from the bus stop. I was left at the bus stop alone.

After about 15 minutes of waiting for the bus, a man in a white Lincoln Crown Victoria pulled next to me, stopped and rolled down his passenger side window to talk to me.

"Hey, it's raining really hard out here! Get in and I'll take you to school," he shouted out.

"No thanks. I'll wait for the bus."

"I'm a police officer! I'm not going to do anything to hurt you, little girl. I just don't want you to be standing out here by yourself in this rain. It's not safe!" he retorted.

I thought to myself, "This loser just will not stop! He will not go away. It is 6:00am, I'm alone at this bus stop and he will not stop! What should I do?" I knew that I had to think fast. At that moment, I was presented with two gates to choose from:

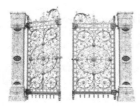 **Gate #1: Promise to harm him in a major way if he doesn't leave me alone.**

By choosing this option, I may be risking my life; however, I may be preventing him from harming someone else. I would also be able to learn more about what he was planning to do and send a strong message to others in the community who may be looking to harm children.

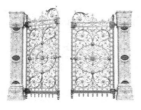 **Gate #2: Run across the street to the gas station and tell the attendant about the strange man.**

By choosing this option, I may be preventing him from harming me or someone else. This option would get another adult involved who would call the police and give them a more detailed description of the strange man than I. This could also prevent the strange man from harming any children in the community while sending a strong message to others who may be thinking about doing so.

Which option would you choose and why? Which option do you think I chose? Can you think of any other options that I could have chosen?

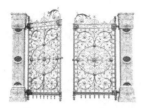 **Gate #1: Promise to harm him in a major way if he doesn't leave me alone.**

By choosing this option, I may be risking my life; however, I may be preventing him from harming someone else. I would also be able to learn more about what he was planning to do and send a strong message to others in the community who may be looking to harm children.

While he was talking, I kept my eyes focused on him and simultaneously opened his gas tank. I removed the cap that covered the gas tank and pulled out my lighter. Then, I flicked the lighter so that the flame was visible and smiled as I spoke these words to him in a calm voice: "If you don't pull off, I'm going to blow you up. Think I'm playing? Look in your mirror."

His eyes widened, and he exclaimed that I was a crazy female dog. Because I saw him put his hand on the gear, I quickly removed my hand from his gas tank as he speed off. Within the next 10 minutes, the bus arrived and I boarded the bus, relaxed in my seat and headed to school.

Later on that evening, Grandma Kali watched the news. I turned my attention towards the television, when the news reporter stated that a little girl who lived around the corner was raped by a man driving a white Lincoln Crown Victoria.

"Grandma! That man tried to take me to school this morning, but he decided to leave me alone. WOW! That's crazy!" I shouted.

"What! Why did he change his mind?" She asked.

"I threatened to kill him if he didn't leave me alone."

After I said this, Grandma Kali shook her head. Then she said, "From now on, you will not be going to the bus stop by yourself. I will take you or your Aunt Leah."

I didn't care whether someone sat with me at the bus stop. I felt like I was already living the life mentioned in the song written by my favorite rapper, Tupac Shakur entitled, "Me against the world." Therefore, I didn't have a problem defending myself against disgusting old men. However, I said, "OK", went upstairs, lay in my bed and drifted to sleep.

I arose the next day, and every other day, eager to go to school. Throughout the remainder of the school year, I drew closer and closer to Ms. Chaney. She became more than just a teacher to me. She was another mother. I could talk to her and she listened. Ms. Chaney would scold me and I would do my best to improve. Unfortunately, after the school year had come to a close, I was confronted with the most disturbing fact: I would have to spend more time at home. Thus, I would have to deal with those annoying girls who lived across the street from me and those trifling women who lived next door to me. I thought to myself, "Here we go again."

Unusual Occurrence

Although I expected to fight all summer, Carissa, Victoria, Korena and I only argued with these two groups of people.

Throughout the summer, the highlight of our days were playing together and going to the mall. We had a great time that summer! At last, the summer was over and it was time to return to school. I was excited!

Finally, I was entering the 10th grade. Thus far, I had been getting good grades and receiving awards. I knew that, in two years, I would graduate high school, move out of my grandma's house, and live on my own. Both my cousin Timina and I looked forward to being able to graduate and live on our own. Although we both traveled separate bus routes to school, today we both arrived on time and waited in the line to enter the school building.

Upon entering the school building and acquiring my schedule, I discovered that Ms. Chaney was still my

English teacher; however, I had a new counselor. Her name was Ms. Sheham. Ms. Sheham was very different from Ms. Frankel, my previous counselor.

Although Ms. Frankel was nice, I never was able to develop a strong bond with her. On the other hand, Ms. Sheham was a very nice, dark-skinned, heavy-set woman with a smile like gold.

Over the school year, I grew to love her. She allowed me to help her in the office during my break time and sometimes during class time: whenever a substitute was in my regular class, or if I was kicked out of my geometry class.

At times that I should have been suspended, she pulled me into her office and talked to me.

One day, she asked me about my mom. Upon hearing the words, "where is your mom?" I cried feverishly in her presence.

Finally, I told her that my mom died of pneumonia when I was seven. I also told her that I had recently found out that my dad was bisexual.

Instead of listening from afar, she wrapped her arms around me and said, "Tresa, it's going to be ok. Things happen to us sometimes, but they just make us stronger. Your grandma has done a marvelous job with you, sweetheart. Any time you want to talk about it, feel free to talk to me. Now, I want you to know that I love you and I don't want to keep seeing you get into trouble in your geometry class."

Although I hated my geometry class, from that day forward, I taught myself geometry and did my best not to disturb the class by asking the teacher questions that she couldn't answer.

As I improved in my geometry class, I learned a lot of information in my health class about the birthing process, sex, and sexually transmitted diseases. The information on sexually transmitted diseases was very interesting to me.

After watching several videos and seeing pictures of the sexually transmitted diseases, I was disgusted with sex in general. However, one topic mentioned during the class intrigued me. It was the topic of sexually transmitted diseases in which no cure exists.

According to the instructor, people who contract these diseases typically die from a common cold or some other trivial illness that the average healthy person can easily overcome. One of the deadly diseases mentioned was AIDS.

I knew that AIDS was a deadly disease, but I didn't know that you could only get it from engaging in one of the following:
1. Having unprotected sex with an infected person.
2. A blood transfusion.
3. Having any open cut that comes into contact with another open cut from someone who was infected with HIV.
4. Sharing needles.

After I had written my notes, I heard my teacher say the following words: "Because HIV is a disease that attacks the immune system, as the immune system is broken down, HIV turns into AIDS and most people who die of AIDS, die from pneumonia or a common cold." I was shocked!

Before I took this health class, I thought that AIDS was a disease that only affected homosexual men;

but, the fact that people who get AIDS die from things like pneumonia bothered me.

Suddenly, the sight of my dad having sex with Uncle Kent flashed before my eyes and I was enraged! I raised my hand to ask a question to confirm that I was taking the proper notes.

I could not believe that people who die from AIDS typically die because of pneumonia or some other common illness. I thought to myself, "My mother died of pneumonia. I wonder if she knew that my dad liked men too. I wonder if she actually had AIDS."

Quickly, my thoughts were interrupted by my teacher's acknowledgement of my raised hand. I asked my teacher more questions about AIDS. He reaffirmed what he had previously said. The sound of his responses to my questions caused me to wonder if I was told the whole truth with regards to my mother's death. Surely, Grandma Kali would not fail to tell me the whole truth about something as serious as this! I decided that when I arrived home, I would ask her.

Then, I did my best to continue to focus on my school work until the bell rang and it was time to go home.

TRUTH ABOUT MOM

I arrived home and patiently waited for Grandma Kali to return home from work. She entered the house and relaxed on the couch for a few minutes. I couldn't take the suspense any longer! I had to know if she told me the whole truth about my mom's death, so I asked her a question.

"Grandma Kali, my mom didn't really die of pneumonia, did she?"

"What are you asking me that for?" she inquired.

"I learned that people who have HIV typically die from things like pneumonia or a common cold when it turns into AIDS. Did she die from AIDS?"

Grandma Kali sighed and said, "When your mother got HIV, it quickly turned into AIDS. Your mom was anemic. This means that she didn't have enough white blood cells to fight off the disease, so it turned into

AIDS fast. Then, she caught pneumonia and died shortly afterwards."

I was devastated! How could she not tell me? Why didn't someone else tell me?

I felt like everyone had lied to me. I felt as if I didn't have any family. Surely, my family wouldn't have done this to me. Here I am, telling people that my mom died from pneumonia and wondering why people looked at me funny after I told them that information, only to later find out that I was lying to them.

Grandma Kali said that the reason she told me that my mom died of pneumonia was because she didn't want me to be treated badly by others, if I shared the truth about my mother's death. She also said that she had me and my siblings tested repeatedly for the disease and I consistently received a negative result.

Because I was so mad, I don't recall anything else from the conversation. For the next six months, I was highly upset with my grandma, aunts, uncles, and especially my dad. I felt as if he had murdered my mom.

I barely held conversations with him when I was over his house, until one day, when I was over my grandfather's house, my dad pulled me to the side and asked me what was going on. He said, "Tresa, you don't talk to me like you used to. Are you angry with me for something?"

I told him that I was angry at him and I missed my mom; however, I didn't tell him what I saw. I wanted him to just tell me his sexuality without that information. After all, kids see their parents engaged in sexual activities all the time; thus, I believed that information was irrelevant.

He tearfully replied, "I miss her too. She was my heart." This statement floored me! I thought to myself, "How was she your heart and you murdered her?" I couldn't take it anymore! I had to know if he was bisexual! I had to know if he had ever told my mom that he liked guys.

As the opportunity presented itself, I promptly asked him, "Are you gay?" I had never seen such pain in my dad's eyes as he uttered the words, "It's complicated. I like men and women. You are my oldest daughter, so since you asked me, I know that you are ready to know. I'm going to tell you everything."

I was hurt and angry. However, I was glad that he took the time to tell me what happened. Some of the details, I did not need to know. In fact, I would have been excited to have never heard them at all; however, they did provide more insight as to how he acquired HIV.

My dad told me that he acquired HIV because he had unprotected sex with so many different men and women during the time he and my mother were together. He also said that my mom was monogamous and he didn't know why he cheated so much. My dad said that he had never told her that he was bisexual; but he believed that she knew.

Then, he wept as he stated that he wished he was dead instead of her. He also told me that he started out as a male dancer at a woman's bar in order to earn some money to help my mom take care of us. However, he transitioned to a homosexual bar because it paid more.

According to him, from that point forward, his job became more than just dancing. He engaged in more sexual practices with other men and women.

To ensure that we talked about everything, he even put in videos of himself male dancing so that I could see what he used to do for a living. He introduced me to people who he had cheated on my mom with whenever they came by his house to visit him. Because my dad had revealed so much information to me, I asked him if he and Uncle Kent was a couple.

He said, "yes, but I wish I had married your mother and not had sex with all those people because she would still be alive. She would still be with me." After my dad said this last statement, he cried profusely.

In the midst of the conversation, I felt bad for my dad. I loved him and I had never seen him in this state. I forgot all about being angry with him. While he was crying, I said to him, "It's ok, daddy. There's nothing we can do about it now. Don't cry. It's going to be ok." Then, I hugged him and said, "I love you dad."

Although I became rather disgusted with male dancing in general, I forgave my father. I realized that his intentions were not to kill my mother, despite the fact that he engaged in irresponsible sexual activities which lead to her death.

I also realized that when you talk about people having sex, it takes two. Because her sexual actions were consensual and she did not insist on using any protection such as condoms, she too played a role in the irresponsible sexual activities which occurred that put her at risk for acquiring HIV.

Until this point, my dad had not told my sister, brother, or I that he was bisexual. He also didn't do anything romantic towards Uncle Kent that would have suggested that the two of them were in any type of relationship. To me, he was living on the down-low in front of his children and another life whenever we were not around.

I loved my dad and he had a great heart. I decided that I'd embrace my dad, regardless of this new information that I had discovered. After all, you only get one mother and one father. Forgiveness is the key to moving from a position of defeat and misery, to a position of victory and power; especially with regards to one's spiritual, emotional, physical, and mental well-being. I am so glad that I forgave him and was able to move forward.

MYSTERY CALL

A few weeks later, I received a phone call from a guy named Mark. He stated that my friend, Victoria, gave him my number and he was interested in getting to know me. I already had an attitude because some random guy called me and my friend didn't even tell me that she gave out my number.

After I got off the phone with him, I went to Victoria's house and knocked on the door.

"Who is it?" someone asked.

"Tresa!" I replied.

At that moment, Victoria's mother opened the door and told her that I was downstairs.

Victoria came to door, smiled and said, "Hey girl."

"Hey lady, so who is Mark?" I asked, as I looked over my glasses at her.

Victoria laughed and said, "He is a friend of this guy I was talking to. He asked me if any of my girls didn't have a man. So I told him about you. He asked me to hook him up, so I gave him your number, but he is cute though."

"Ok, so what does he look like?" I asked.

"He is light skinned, with a 360 cut, perfect smile and muscles."

"What? Alright then, thanks for the hook up. We are supposed to see each other in a few weeks," I replied. "No problem girl."

As the weeks went by, I talked with Mark for hours each day. I really liked him.

Finally, the day had arrived when Mark and I would meet at Victoria's house. While at her house, Victoria, Carissa, and I stood on the porch laughing and just having a good time.

After about two hours, a man driving a vehicle parallel parked on the street in front of Victoria's house. From the porch, I looked into the car and saw a light-skinned guy with a 360 cut who appeared to be tall, sitting in the passenger seat.

"Is that him?" I asked with great anticipation of a favorable response from Victoria.

"Uh, no that's the guy I'm talking to," Victoria said.

Suddenly, a short, dark-skinned guy got out of the driver's seat. I turned and furiously glared at Victoria. She laughed and said, "I thought he was light skinned, with a 360 cut, tall with muscles. It was dark out! Ha. Ha. Ha. I'm sorry girl."

Although I was upset with my friend for giving me faulty information, the fact that Mark did not look like the description was irrelevant. I had already decided that I really liked Mark. The more we talked and spent time together, the closer Mark and I were drawn to one another.

EMOTIONAL EXPLOSION

In fact, the closer we became to one another, the more I listened to the advice that Mark gave me; especially during the times that I was so angry that I could barely think straight. On this particular day, I experienced one of those times.

My sister informed me that Laicey and her sister had tried to jump her after school. I was so furious! I was tired of arguing and fighting these girls! Determined to get to the main reason for the tension between Laicey and my sister, I decided to ask Laicey why she didn't like my sister.

Before going to Laicey's house to ask her why she didn't like my sister, I walked down to Carissa's house to talk to her about it.

While we were talking, I noticed that Laicey and Hattie were walking towards us on the opposite side of the street. Immediately, I said to Carissa, "I'm about to go over there and just talk to her because this doesn't make any sense."

"You ain't goin by yourself! I'm going with you," Carissa stated.

After we crossed the street, I talked to Laicey. At first, Laicey answered my questions and we were having a decent conversation. However, while we were talking, Laicey's other sisters and several of my relatives arrived. After her oldest sister arrived, Laicey yelled and acted as if she was ready to fight me. Then, Laicey's oldest sister jumped in front of her, walked around the circle and stepped in front of my relatives and friends, then put her finger on their foreheads and called them female dogs. Finally, she got to me. Then, she attempted to perform the same action towards me that he done to my relatives.

Instantly, I was presented with two gates to choose from with regards to accessing a life that I would live. That life could either be a life of hell or of prosperity. The gates and the actions within them are as follows:

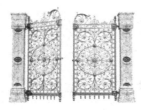 **Gate #1: Diffuse the situation by encouraging my family and friends to walk away from Laicey's 21 year old sister.**

By choosing this option, I may be risking my reputation; however, I would be ensuring that my family and friends are not harmed by being involved in a fight.

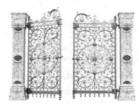 **Gate #2: Respond with violence.**

By choosing this option, I would have an opportunity to teach her a lesson while simultaneously, defending my family. This decision indicated that I didn't care about the consequences associated with my actions. I just wanted her to know who was truly a "boss".

Which choice would you choose? Which gate do you think I chose to unlock and open? Are there any other options to this situation available? What could have prevented me from encountering this situation in the first place? What would you do differently? As you turn the page, you will discover which gate I chose to unlock.

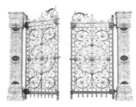

Gate #2: Respond with violence.

By choosing this option, I would have an opportunity to teach her a lesson while simultaneously, defending my family. This decision indicated that I didn't care about the consequences associated with my actions. I just wanted her to know who was truly a "boss".

As she walked closer to me, all I saw was red. When she was within arm's reach, she attempted to put her index finger on my forehead and call me a female dog. Yet, I was determined not to allow her to disrespect me in that manner.

Thus, I reached into my pocket, pulled out my box cutter, then moved as close to her as I could and motioned to cut out her stomach with the blade. She was pregnant! Before I could reach her stomach, my sister, cousins, and friends all pulled on one of my arms in order to ensure that I did not give Dawn an instant abortion. In unison, they pulled me as hard as they could in order to get me to stop.

Once my family and friends dragged me across the street, I noticed that all of the girls who were previously attempting to fight us walked back home. I tried to break free in order to follow through on my plans, but I couldn't.

I was so angry that I yelled the following phrase to all of those girls: "All y'all dying tonight!" as I traveled home.

Upon arriving home, I opened the door and ran up the stairs to use the telephone. I called my ex-boyfriend.

Although we were not a couple, he was a good friend of mine. I called him because I knew that he still had guns, grenades, and wild animals; such as his pet panther. All of those items would help me accomplish my goal of annihilating those girls who had disrespected me.

"Hey, what's up?" he asked.

"I'm pissed off! I need you to drive by this house and blow it up with two grenades!"

"What? What's wrong? I'll do that baby, but I haven't ever heard you talk like that. What happened?" he asked in a concerned manner.

"I don't even want to talk about it no more. How soon can you make this happen, man?"

"Just give me the address and I'll be on my way," he replied.

By the time I gave him the address, my sister ran upstairs.

"Who was that? Who you giving their address to?" she asked.

While she was talking, I pressed play on my stereo in order to listen to one of my favorite songs titled, "I hit em up" by Tupac Shakur.

When she noticed that I was ignoring her, she said things like, "It's not that serious Tresa! For real, who is going over there? What they gone do?"

I was still so consumed by rage. Immediately, I called another male friend of mine that I knew had just gotten out of jail, and asked him to drive by the house first to shoot it up.

At my request, he replied, "Man, I got you baby girl. What time do you need me to do it?"

"Within the next thirty minutes, because I'm having it blown away afterwards."

"Tresa!" Grandma Kali yelled, "Come here!"

I ran down the stairs to see what she wanted. Much to my surprise, the girls' mother was at the front door.

"Did you tell her daughters that they were all going to die tonight?" Grandma Kali asked, as she looked at me with utter disdain.

After I responded to this question with a "Yes," I turned towards their mother and said, "You tell them I meant what I said!"

Grandma Kali was so pissed off that she slapped me and demanded that I apologize to their mother.

I refused. With each refusal, I received another slap until she realized that I was not going to apologize.

Then she said, "Go to your room!" I ran back upstairs more upset than I was before this encounter.

When I entered my room, huffing and cracking my knuckles, my sister Korena said, "Tresa, kids live in that house!"

"I don't care! It's not my fault! She should have thought about that before she did what she did!" I yelled.

"Don't kill the kids! They didn't do nothing to you."

I tuned her out and continued to listen to my music. Suddenly, I noticed that 15 minutes had already passed.

The song had ended and I had calmed down. At that moment, I thought about what my sister said: "kids live in that house. Don't kill the kids!" At once, I called my male friend who was supposed to shoot the house up for me.

"What's good love? I'm on my way," he answered.

"No, don't do it man. Kids live in that house. Never mind," I said.

"Are you sure, because I am not that far away from the house?" he said.

"I am sure."

"Ok sweetie. You know I got yo back right?" he asked. "Yes. By the way, thanks for being willing, man."

Afterwards, we said goodbye and I called my ex-boyfriend back to cancel my previously scheduled massacre. He answered the phone as well. I told him that I no longer needed him to throw grenades into the house because there was kids living there and they didn't do anything wrong.

"You sure babe? I was just packing my stuff and getting ready to head ova dare," he said.

"Yes, I'm sure. Thanks anyways."

I hung up the phone and sat in my room silently. While sitting on my bed, I wrote poems in order to relax at a faster rate. I thought to myself, "I hate when people 'make' me this angry!" as I laid down upon my bed and took a nap.

After I had awakened from my rest, I called Mark to talk to him about it. Mark and I were moving closer towards being in a relationship.

I told him everything that happened. Much to my surprise, he didn't say, "Girl you crazy!"

Instead, he said, "Bay, you really need to control your anger. I'm not trying to lose you over something stupid like 'someone called you out of your name or pushed you'. Nobody can make you angry. It's a choice."

His last statement consistently rang in my head during our conversation, in conjunction with the scriptures that I had read over the years, related to this emotion. Mark and I continued to talk. Eventually, I was no longer upset about what happened and we ended our conversation. I decided to read a book written by my favorite author and go to sleep.

Turning Point: 'Reverse Psychology' at its best

The next day, I arose and got ready to go outside. Grandma Kali stopped me at the door with the following statement: "Tresa, I know you are going to fight somebody today, but can you at least tell an adult or somebody first?"

As I listened to those words come from Grandma Kali's mouth, I felt like daggers were thrown through my heart. I thought to myself, "Did she give up on me? She normally says "be good" or "have fun," but now she gone tell me what I'm gone do. She has been one of the few people who always believed that I could do anything and she gone say something to me like this! You know what? I don't have to fight today. As a matter of fact, I'll show her. I'm not going to have any fights today. No not one!"

Immediately, I went outside. When the same people attempted to start an argument with me, I ignored them. I said to myself, "Not today, but if they keep this up, tomorrow it's a wrap!"

Much to my surprise, I was able to get through an entire day without fighting or arguing with anyone. It was at that moment that I realized that I had the power to control my actions. Yes, people attempted to get negative reactions out of me, but I refused to give them any. I was fully in control.

From that day forward, the frequency of my experiences in altercations had decreased. I realized that no one could 'make' me do anything. How I act is a choice, and I have the right to make whatever choices I want to make. With every choice, there are by-products or consequences of that choice. I can choose what I am willing to experience because they coincide with the actions that I make.

Thus, the phrase "For every action there is a reaction, and I can choose the type of reactions that I want to experience," became a decision-making reference tool for me.

I decided to engage in the process of gaining more self-control, which would lead to freedom from anger and rage, by continuing to read the Holy Bible, putting into action the scriptures that I had learned and my reference tool. I thought to myself, "This upcoming weekend would be a good time to start using these things that I have learned to control myself; especially since I'm going over my dad's house."

Some Things Should Not Be Repeated

While traveling to my dad's house, I thought about the fact that Uncle Roland was going to be there. I really didn't like him. Despite my feelings about him, I decided to do my best to at least be cordial with him and not allow anger to overtake me.

I also decided that I will not attempt to kill him anymore; especially since I kept hearing the scripture, "thou shall not kill," each time I attempted to do so.

I still felt uneasy around him; however, I no longer was instantly enraged at the sight of him. When I saw him, instead of being so angry that I stared at him as if death rays were firing from my eyes; my cousins and I played and just had a wonderful time. The next day; however, was a little different.

Although the usual activities occurred, Uncle Kent, who was also known as Lenny, told me that my dad said that he didn't believe that Uncle Roland had molested me. I was hurt! I could not believe what I was hearing! Part of me wanted to go and confront my dad about what Lenny had told me. However, the other part of me just wanted to discontinue all contact with my dad. I was livid! I hadn't lied to him before, why would he think that I would lie to him about something as serious as this?

Because I was angry with my dad, I avoided him. I played with all of my cousins and did my best to not have extensive conversations with him. I was disgusted. After I had forgiven him for engaging in actions that caused my mother's death, how dare he treat me like this? I thought we were closer than that.

Towards the end of my 11th grade year of school, I decided to let it go. Since I couldn't change the way my dad felt about the information he received, I believed that it was time for me to try to forget about it and focus on my senior year in high school.

Senior Year

Finally, it was my senior year! I was so excited! For years, I had planned to move out of Grandma Kali's house and go to college. In fact, while in second grade, I said that I will go to either Starlight High School or John Paul High School.

I was graduating from Starlight High School. My desires were finally manifesting; with the exception of my desire to keep my English teacher from my previous two years in high school.

During my last year of high school, I had a different teacher for English. Her name was Ms. Tyson. She was known to be very strict; however, she was very good at what she did best: teach. One of her classroom rules drove me crazy! It was the rule, "all for one and one for all."

The application of this rule meant that if 'someone' in the class did not stop behaving in an inappropriate manner, 'everyone' in the class would have to write a research paper about whatever 'we' failed to do as a group.

For example, let's say it's Monday and she said, "Stop talking." If one person in the class continued to talk after she counted to three, it indicated that, as a group, 'we' failed to comply with her request. Thus, 'we' would be required to submit a double-spaced research paper with one inch margins on the topic: "Why is it important for students to be silent while the teacher is talking?" Everyone in the class would also be required to use at least one scholarly source while answering this question.

At one point, I felt as if we had to write papers everyday because one student just wouldn't quit! Not only did we have to write the papers, we were required to turn them in. In fact, Ms. Tyson actually graded those assignments. If you didn't do the assignment, it would hurt your grade, because it became an actual assignment.

Eventually, it became easy for me to complete the task. Fortunately, the student who consistently caused the entire class to write these papers had also matured towards the middle of the semester. Therefore, our class was not required to write as many research papers as we did in the beginning of the semester.

Over the school year, I developed a loving relationship with Ms. Tyson as well. We were so close that I called her Aunt Tyson. Before and after class, she listened to me and I listened to her as we discussed my personal struggles.

One day, she informed me that she was also a professor at Main State University. When I asked her why she punished everyone for one person's actions, her response was: "You are all one in my eyes". To her, we were a team. Whenever she had to address us in meetings, she referred to us as her 7th hour class; thus, we were one.

She also stated that the assignments had multiple purposes. One of the purposes was to stop us from misbehaving in class. The other purpose was to develop our writing and research skills in order to prepare us for college. Ms. Tyson often proclaimed that all of us were going to college. And I believed her.

It was a matter of time before my belief would be challenged by the financial status of my family. Despite the challenge, Grandma Kali was ready to equip me to conquer it.

One day Grandma Kali said, "Tresa, you're going to college; but, I can't afford to pay for it, so you need to figure out how to get there, legally. You are a great writer and you are very creative. You need to think of a way to get somebody else to pay for you to go to college. Maybe you can get some scholarships. You figure it out; but you're going to college."

I decided to use what I had learned when I was much younger: start my own business.

During this period of my life, Mark asked me to marry him. I said, "Yes" then later in the year we launched a business called Surprising Gifts and Creations. Mark taught me how to use Adobe Photoshop, Dreamweaver, and Adobe Illustrator.

As my skills sharpened, I marketed the organization to teachers and classmates in my school. Some of the things I designed included Homecoming

Queen Posters, poems and cards. We sold each poster for $10-$15. We took advantage of each holiday by using not only our graphic abilities, but also my poetic abilities.

For example, on Valentine's Day, I told people that if they informed me of how they felt about a person, I would create a personalized poem that reflected their thoughts. I also allowed them to choose decorative paper to be used for the placement of the poem.

If they wanted the poems to be framed, the cost was $5 each. If they wanted both the poem to be framed and me to personally deliver the gift to the person, the cost was $7 each. If they wanted the poem to be framed and delivered with flowers and a bear to the person of their choice, the cost was $10 each.

Eventually, I earned enough money to pay for all of the things I needed for prom and saved some money to help pay for a few of my books upon entering my first semester in college.

Although it was nice to be able to pay for prom and pay for some of my books once I entered college, the issue regarding how I was going to pay for college remained present. My mom didn't leave me any money after she died. Also, my dad simply could not afford to pay for me to go to college. I knew that I had to do something. At that moment, I was presented with two gates to a potential life:

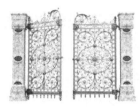 **Gate #1: Contact people I knew that sold drugs and ask them if I could sell some for a little while until I earned enough money to pay for college.**

By choosing this option, I would go against everything I believed with regards to drugs; however, I would be able to get enough money to afford to pay for college so that my education wasn't a burden on Grandma Kali.

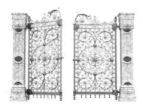 **Gate #2: Seek wise counsel
and do what they say.**

By choosing this option, I would be able to avoid the
potential of going to jail, while increasing my chances of
getting the money I needed to pay for college. This
would ensure that my education was not a burden on
Grandma Kali, who had already sacrificed her life to
take care of me.

Which gate do you believe I opened? What are the
consequences associated with choosing to open each
gate? Which option would you choose and why?

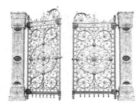 **Gate #2: Seek wise counsel and do what they say.**

By choosing this option, I would be able to avoid the potential of going to jail, while increasing my chances of getting the money I needed to pay for college. This would ensure that my education was not a burden on Grandma Kali - who had already sacrificed her life to take care of me.

I went into Ms. Sheham's office and spoke to her about the situation. She told me all about scholarships and grants.

She said, "Tresa, you have been involved in a lot of student organizations and your grades are really good. Therefore, you have a really good chance of getting all the scholarships that you need to go to school. If you write one really good 500 word essay, you could apply for multiple scholarships using that essay. You have to make sure that you slightly alter the essay by personalizing it and answering the questions each scholarship asks. Be sure to mention what you plan to do with their money," she explained.

Ms. Sheham continued to inform me of the process to applying for scholarships by saying, "Scholarships are like business deals. No one wants to randomly invest their time or money without being sure that they will receive a return on their investment."

She also mentioned to me that she was on a scholarship judging committee; thus, she knew what it would take for me to acquire scholarships.

Without reservation, she told me the things that scholarship judging committees look for, when they attempt to determine who they will select to receive their scholarship.

These things included: professionalism, creativity and originality. According to Ms. Sheham, the most important thing that anyone could do when applying for scholarships is to 'stand out'.

You stood out by having an interesting, grammatically error free essay, that demonstrated your creative abilities, and answered the question or questions asked of you. I took detailed notes regarding what must be included in this major essay and how to stand out.

After meeting with Ms. Sheham, I went to acquire more advice from one of my favorite teachers: Ms. Tyson. She advised me to have my essays proofread prior to submitting them. She also told me that she would be willing to proofread my essays.

After I completed my first essay, I took it to Ms. Tyson and asked her to proofread it. She seemed shocked by my request. Ms. Tyson said that she had given many students the option of her proofreading their essays; however, I was one of the few who had taken her offer.

She proofread my essay and returned it to me. Each correction that she suggested, I made.

One of the essays she proofread was the one I gave to the Admissions Representative from the University of Talver (U of T), who came to visit my school.

This essay was for a scholarship that would cover five years tuition and fees at the U of T. The name of the scholarship was the Distinguished Student Leader Scholarship.

Because I knew the representative was coming to my school that day, I dressed in a black suit, typed the admissions application in advance, placed the essay on decorative paper, and put the answers to the information U of T requested on the application into a one page resume format.

When it was my turn to speak with the representative, I looked him in the eyes, smiled, and briefly told him about myself. Then, I gave him a copy of my application and informed him that I included a one page resume which summarized my qualifications for admission. He said that he hadn't met a student as professional as I was, and he would definitely turn in my admissions and scholarship applications.

All of these actions paid off because I received the Distinguished Student Leader Scholarship (DSL).

Although I received the DSL Scholarship, I did not stop applying for scholarships. I applied for 13 other scholarships.

By graduation, I had received five of those scholarships. My scholarship money was valued at over $45,000.

I had also been accepted to the University of Talver and a few other universities. Although my ACT score was only a 19, which was lower than the school required for admission, my grade point average was a 3.88. This grade point average was higher than the school's requirement for admission.

As a result, I was admitted to the University of Talver through the Support Services department. If I had said to myself, "I don't have the ACT score necessary, so I don't qualify for this college," then I wouldn't have applied to the school. Had I failed to apply, I would have missed an opportunity to acquire the five year tuition and fees paid scholarship.

Because I submitted the application, despite these facts, it indicated that I was led by my faith, instead of my issues. As a result of operating in this manner, I gained admission into the college of my choice.

Ms. Sheham was the one who told me to apply despite my short-comings, I am forever grateful to her for encouraging me to refuse to allow a low ACT score to stop me from applying to colleges. She said that colleges would review all aspects of a student's achievement, both academic and extracurricular, in order to make their admissions decisions.

Finally I graduated from high school. Grandma Kali and all of the rest of my close relatives attended my graduation. My dad was on time for my graduation and I was excited about it! My graduation from high school launched the next period of my life: college.

Epilogue: College and the Conclusion of the Matter

While I was in college, I met some good friends. I also continued to receive scholarships and other awards.

The day I graduated from the University of Talver with honors in psychology and communications, Mark brought my dad with him to the graduation. To my surprise, he had a gift with him: a bouquet of yellow roses. I was grateful for the gift. It was my favorite flower, but I did not particularly like yellow roses. I wondered why he chose to purchase yellow roses for me.

My thoughts were interrupted by his statement, "Tresa, I am so proud of you! Although I know that the yellow rose is not your favorite color rose, I am giving you yellow roses because it was your mother's favorite. I never had a chance to buy them for her. You look so much like her. I am giving them to you instead. I love you."

After hearing his explanation, I cried tears of joy. How thoughtful! My dad definitely had a big heart. I embraced him and continued to receive the other bouquets of roses my other relatives blessed me with that day. Afterwards, I went home, put all of my flowers in water then attended my graduation party with my sister and close friend, Trina, from college.

Eventually, Mark and I grew apart and I drew closer to God after joining Spirit & Honesty Christian Ministries. I went on to obtain more awards and acquired a Master of Social Work degree from the University of Talver. I also traveled to various different high schools and middle schools and delivered presentations.

During my travels, I realized that I loved to share information with people and see it change the lives of those who utilized it.

In 2009, under the direction of Holy Spirit, I decided to launch "It's Time Enterprises" as my vehicle to empower others to push beyond the barriers they face in life and possess their dreams. Approximately two years later, Grandma Kali had several heart attacks, with other complications, and my dad's medical condition also got worst. Although I was attempting to finish my newest master's degree in General Administration from Central Hanson University, the pressure was so intense that I found it difficult to focus on my coursework.

One day, the Lord led me to have a serious talk with my dad. During this conversation, I told him how I felt about his decision not to believe me when I told him what had happened to me when I was a child. We also discussed every issue related to my mom's death.

As a result of this discussion, I gained new insight with regards to his actions. I soon realized that things were not as they seemed. He had been hurting ever since her death and hearing the information about what happened to me. I found out that he also was molested by his uncle and he simply didn't know what to do with the information I told him.

I forgave him again and asked him to forgive me for failing to be a better daughter to him. He told me that he forgave me as well; but to him, I was always a great daughter.

During this conversation, I was presented with an opportunity to lead my father into a prayer of repentance. He repented and rededicated his life to Christ upon his confession of faith and acceptance of Jesus Christ as his Lord and Savior.

Shortly afterwards, he died. I preached his eulogy and was responsible for all of the events surrounding his burial. Although I felt like a wrecking ball had beaten my heart, I was so grateful that he was not suffering anymore. It broke my heart to see my father deteriorate throughout the years.

The same year I was dealing with the loss of my father, Grandma Kali was having heart surgery. As a result of prayer, God blessed Grandma Kali to live and survive her heart surgery, despite what the doctor's had previously said.

I said all of this to let you know that with God, all things are possible. You may have made errors in your life by opening and entering the wrong gates, as I did in the beginning. However, as long as you have breath in your body, another gate to life will be presented before you. Seek wise counsel to ensure that you choose the right gate. Heed the words of wisdom that come from the wise. Know that if you had made the right choices all by yourself, you wouldn't have continued to get the undesirable results that you keep getting in your life.

I say to you the same message that Grandma Kali always said to me, "Don't be stupid all your life. At some point, get a clue."

You choose the life that you shall experience. Decide what type of life you desire to live and make the necessary changes today in order to live that life.

Remember, as you take one step towards your destiny, God will take three. Allow Him to help you select the right gate; by heeding the wisdom from his chosen vessels. Everyday wisdom speaks. Can you hear her? It's time for you to open the right gate in order to gain access to greatness. Your destiny is waiting on you! Open the right gate to life and experience it.

About the Author

"Introducing the heavyweight champion of the world: Latresa Rice!" When people think of heavyweight champions, they think of boxers who have consistently defeated their opponents.

Although she isn't an actual boxer, her life reflects that of a heavyweight champion.

Throughout her life, Ms. Rice has come against emotional, physical, financial, socioeconomic, and other barriers to her successful possession of her dreams. However, she has, and continues to annihilate them all.

From overcoming the emotional trauma she experienced after discovering the truth regarding her mother's death from AIDS and father's sexuality, to learning how to use the skills she possess' to obtain the finances she needs to be successful, Ms. Rice stands as an example of an undefeated heavyweight champion.

Since 2000, she has been travelling to elementary, middle, and high schools throughout Wayne and Oakland County: delivering inspiring, captivating, empowering and entertaining (I.C.E.E.) speeches to youth. The purpose of these speeches was to empower the youth to push beyond the barriers they face in life and possess their dreams.

Ms. Rice has also empowered women within drug treatment facilities, young adults in alternative schools, and other underprivileged individuals, through the delivery of her power-packed presentations.

These presentations include "Thank You Haters", "Employees Wanted," "Sex & Truth", "College Explosion," and "Young Queens".

Furthermore, Ms. Rice is a songwriter and singer. Her first song was a ringtone called, "Thank You Haters," which is available for only 99 cents on cdbaby.com, amazon.com, itunes.com, and many more.

Although she is a very talented young woman, she also is fun to be around and loves to relax by water.

Currently, Ms. Rice resides in the heart of the city of Detroit. Uniquely positioned to write such a life altering book, Ms. Rice shines as her life unfolds before your eyes in her first book titled, 'Gate to Life: You Choose the Life that You Shall Experience'.

For more information regarding how you can purchase more copies of this book, or if you would like your audience to not only receive information that will propel them into their glorious destiny, but embark on an experience unmatched by any other, stop what you are doing, pick up the phone, and call Ms. Rice at 313-799-4864, or email her at lrice@itewisdom.com to book her for your event today!

Acknowledgement

First and foremost, I thank you God, the Father, for calling me out of darkness into your marvelous light.

I thank you God, the Son (Jesus Christ), for shedding your precious blood that I may have an opportunity to have everlasting life.

I thank you God, Holy Spirit, for ordering my steps, and empowering me to be able to finish this book, despite the barriers presented by the enemy.

Oh blessed Trinity, you are three forms wrapped in one called God just as water is a gas (two parts Hydrogen, and one Oxygen), a liquid (a wet substance), and a solid (an ice cube). I thank you for your love and guidance.

To Bishop James A. Williams II., and Pastor Kelli R. Williams of Spirit & Truth Christian Ministries, thank you for always being so supportive. You are phenomenal spiritual parents.

Thank you Shenita Miller for consistently pushing me to finish this book, and encouraging me to pursue every vision that God has given me.

Thank you Melissa Dunmore for walking with me throughout my childhood and during this present time. I appreciate all of your encouragement to finish this book.

Thank you Chariece Cylar, for all the laughs and fun times over the years.

Thank you Jennifer Tucker for your editing expertise, laughs, and encouragement.

Thank you Brandon Marsh for being such a supportive and encouraging person. During my weakest moments, God blessed you to encourage me to continue to pursue my destiny with regards to this book and my vision for It's Time Enterprises. I am so grateful for your words of encouragement and advice.

Thank You Shirley Hogsett of Destiny Speaks Speakers Bureau for all of your advice and direction regarding the creation, marketing, and publishing of this book.

I couldn't have done this without each of you. I love you all very much!

To my brother (Daron Rice Sr.), sister (Latosha Rice), and cousin (Shanita Alston), I love you very much. Thank you for listening and encouraging me to complete this book. You've seen my struggles as well as my victories. I pray that I will live my life to such an extent, that it stands as an example for you to use as you pursue and accomplish your dreams. I'm looking forward to watching each of you walk in your destiny.

To Mr. Dwayne Flowers Sr. and Mrs. Cassandra Flowers, Pastor Deborah Satterwhite, and Mr. Edward Satterwhite, thank you for all of your love and encouragement. I love and appreciate you.

To Mr. William Keener, thank you for all of your support, love, and encouragement. I couldn't have done this without you. I love you with all of my heart.

All praises to God for allowing both my mother (Arletta Rice) and my father (Reuben Spicer) to no longer suffer with AIDS and return to Him. I love and miss them both so much.

To my lovely grandmother (Minnie Rice), I thank you for all of your instruction, guidance, love, and correction. You are my greatest inspiration. I desire to be as strong and loving as you. Because of you, I am the woman that I am today. Words couldn't fully express how grateful I am for your decision to sacrifice yourself that my sister, brother and I may have an opportunity to flourish in life. I LOVE YOU GRANDMA!!!!!

To all of you, who have purchased this book, thank you for your support. May God bless you abundantly. Always remember that gates to life are presented before you every day. You have the power to choose the life that you shall experience by walking through the right gate that is presented before you and using your keys, which are your words and your actions, to gain entrance.

Choose life and not death. No matter what you have been through, there is always someone else who has been through worse. The mere fact that you are still living means that you have not reached your destiny; thus, you still have time to open the right gate and possess your dreams.

Open that gate today or continue to walk the
path that does not lead to prosperity. The choice is yours.